The Other Side of Knowing

The Other Side of Knowing

Searching for Truth and Peace
during World War II and Its Aftermath

By Margit Seifried Benton

ISBN: 978-1508670469

Printed by CreateSpace, An Amazon.com Company

Edited by Mary B. Johnston of Wordworks
www.marywordworks.com

Cover and Book design by Laura Pierce Design
www.laurapiercedesign.com

This book is dedicated to the silent dead beneath a field of clover near Pohořelice in southern Moravia, Czech Republic. Their voices were not allowed to be heard.

"The most grievous violation of . . . any human right is to deprive populations of their right to occupy the country where they live by compelling them to live elsewhere. The fact that the victorious powers decided at the end of World War II to impose this fate on hundreds of thousands of human beings and, what is more, in a most cruel manner, shows how little they were aware of the challenge facing them, namely, to re-establish prosperity and, as far as possible, the rule of law."

Albert Schweitzer upon accepting the Nobel Peace Prize in Oslo, Norway, on November 4, 1954.

Table of Contents

Acknowledgements

WITHOUT THE ENCOURAGEMENT of my siblings and friends I would have never started writing my story. Being foreign born, I did not trust my English language skills. It was not until I met Mary Johnston, an editor and writing coach who took on the challenge of pulling together my family history and giving it the direction it needed, that I began writing in earnest. I am very grateful to her. I also would like to thank my friend Susan Vaughan for her continued help and reassurance; whenever I felt like giving up, she would say, "You need to share the story of the struggles you endured and the faith in God that you developed along the way."

Special thanks also go to Chris Cooper, Suzan Wilson, Linda Humphrey, Lindsey Johnson, Alice-Anne Holmquist and Christopher Ian Matt for their invaluable insights and advice.

I thank my parents for my life and for naming me after my older sister Margita, who died before I was born. I have lived my life in a way that I hope fulfilled my own life's mission as well as hers. I also thank my siblings for their confidence that I could do justice to our family's story.

Finally, I would like to thank God for letting me fulfill the promise of writing the story of my people.

Preface

THE SCARS OF World War II cut deeply across the globe. Millions of soldiers and countless civilians perished by the bullet and the bomb. Many of Europe's beautiful cities were damaged, some decimated. Governments and economies faltered and struggled to recover; some still haven't.

The immeasurable pain borne by Jews as well as soldiers and civilians across Europe and the Pacific cannot be measured with statistics. It is their stories—captured in memoirs, movies, photographs and music—that have given voice and meaning to their suffering. But there is one group whose story has not been told.

An estimated fifteen million ethnic Germans (*Volksdeutsche*)—Germans who lived outside of Germany—became victims of a revenge-driven, nationalistic cleansing after the war ended. They were forced out of their homelands of Poland, Hungary, Yugoslavia, and Czechoslovakia—all countries that once comprised the Austro-Hungarian Empire where Germans had lived for centuries.

More than two million were killed with many more unaccounted for. Over eight hundred thousand were abducted and dragged into labor camps in Siberia while thousands more were jailed for crimes they did not commit. Ethnic Germans took the blows of a violent backlash against all Germans, regardless of their national citizenry or political allegiance.

Images of Nazi cruelty have populated magazines and history books for decades. They have fueled discussions, debates, sympathy, and symbolism for the entire world, but nothing has been presented to reveal the explosive anger levied against the *Volksdeutsche*. Their story, the final evil dust that settled after the rise and fall of the

Third Reich, is an account of rejection, forced expulsion, cruelty, misery, and death.

These were my people.

Though German is my mother tongue, my homeland is the former Czechoslovakia, my family's home country for centuries; it was the country that, once the war was over, wanted nothing to do with anyone who spoke Hitler's language.

Although we had never lived in Germany, the Czechs, our countrymen, were determined that we return "home." West Germany's bombed-out cities and its crushed economy were not fertile ground for anybody. Nevertheless, it is where my parents and I were sent to live.

The families we lived with did not want us; we were intruders. We lived apart, yet under the same roof. Regardless of our training and education, we were mocked publicly and given menial labor for which we were not paid. We scraped the floors and the fields for our survival, grateful for a room, food, and any kind word.

Decades passed before the healing could begin. My parents passed away without ever seeing their homeland again. I left Germany in search of the childhood I had lost. The broken pieces of my life eventually came together after a forty-five year long journey that led me to find a new home and new meaning for my life.

Introduction

PAINFUL MEMORIES FLOODED my mind, as I sat where
I had seen and smelled so much sickness and death. Here, at the
former State Agricultural Experimental Station in Pohořelice, the
most southern village in Moravia only a few miles from the border
between Czechoslovakia and Austria, I witnessed evil's dark hand.
I was only fifteen—without a home or a homeland. I lived on one
bowl of soup a day. The huge storage buildings, where Mother and I
slept in the spring of 1945, were still visible in the distance. The field
once covered with the stench of hurriedly buried corpses was now
a deep green field of clover, lush and gently swaying in the morning
breeze. A few feet away from me stood a tall steel cross and a memorial for those who had lost their lives.

On the bench next to me sat a young woman. She was too
young to have witnessed what had happened here so long ago. I
nodded a greeting and we introduced ourselves. "No," she responded to my question about what brought her here. "I don't have family
buried here, but I know the story." Pointing towards the storage
buildings in the distance, I said, "I know the story too. I lived it." I
looked at the young woman for her reaction and saw sympathy and
understanding in her eyes. I continued, "Death waited outside our
door during the day and entered each night. Broken bodies were
hauled away in darkness and buried carelessly in this field. Here
I planted a question in my heart so powerful that it has haunted
me ever since. Now that the Iron Curtain has come down and the
borders have opened, I have come all the way from America to find
the answer." She looked at me and asked, "Do you mind sharing
your question with me?"

Relieved to have an audience and to be where I knew I needed
to be, I uttered the question that I had never said aloud that had

haunted me for years: "Is the torture and killing of innocent people forgivable by God?"

A Humble but Happy Home

FOR MANY YEARS I tried not to think about the question that weighed so heavily on my heart, for to wonder about God's willingness to forgive evildoers meant thinking about death, depravity, and violence.

When Mother and I left the camp in Pohořelice and traveled by truck back home to Brno[1], over the same road we had only a week before walked with thousands of exhausted and dying people, I received a spiritual impression that told me "Margit, be at peace, for I have everything under control." I did not understand the message at that time, but felt a sudden calm come over me.

Slowly, I learned to accept the degradation I had experienced, however, for me to fully understand and accept the Lord's message took much longer. In 1981, I became a member of The Church of Jesus Christ of Latter-day Saints. I then began to understand God's ways and teachings; yet still did not have an answer to my questions about the suffering I had witnessed and experienced and the lack of meaning and love I felt in my own life. When the Iron Curtain came down in 1989 and the borders with the West opened, I received promptings to return to Pohořelice, where I knew God would answer my question about the war's injustices. In 1991 I was able to follow these promptings.

There was another question to which I *did* have an answer: How did I come to suffer the fate I did? In other words, how did I come to be an ethnic German? My paternal grandfather came as

---

1   Brno is the city's Czech name. Between 1939 and 1945, when Czechoslovakia became the Protectorate of the German Reich, the city was called Brünn.

a merchant from Holzhäusel in upper Austria and settled in Brno before the turn of the century, hoping to expand his furniture business. My mother's family came from Poland. As farmers, they too came to the area hoping to benefit from the rich soil of Moravia's countryside. Both families had learned of the industrial growth in this part of the Austro-Hungarian Empire and were eager to be part of that new developing energy; but Austria and Germany's defeat in World War I crushed their dreams of a prosperous future. The empire, which comprised all of Central Europe, was broken up along ethnic lines.

Pockets of German-speaking people were stranded socially and politically in what became Czechoslovakia in 1918, the very year my parents were married. During the two decades between World War I and II, they built a home and raised a family. Although Czechoslovakia[2] prospered economically, tension mounted in the interior of the country as well as in the Sudetenland, the German name used in the first half of the twentieth century for the western regions of Czechoslovakia inhabited mostly by ethnic Germans. The cause of the tension? The Czech government was violating the League of Nations' treaties that had ensured legal parity and protection of minorities.

Father had witnessed these violations firsthand. He was eager to pursue a career in the wholesale textile business after he finished his technical training and apprenticeship with a large company in 1914. However, after he returned from the war, having fought Austria's losing battles, he was offered only a ground-level sales position, the starting salary of which made it difficult to meet the needs of his growing family. Though no salesman knew his trade better, Father was never promoted to department manager—not because he lacked knowledge or company loyalty, but because of his ethnicity. Discrimination against Germans, whose country had dealt such

2   The name of my homeland has changed multiple times. In this memoir I will simply refer to it as Czechoslovakia.

destructive blows for four devastating years, was common in the civil service as well as the private sector throughout Czechoslovakia.

The first few years of my parents' married life were particularly difficult, but not just for economic reasons. In 1922 their first child, two-year-old Margita, died of scarlet fever. My parents were devastated. In 1924, however, Lilli was born, followed by Erwin two years later. I came along on Easter in 1930. To overcome the economically difficult times, Mother's brother Theodore, who had a large farm outside the city, supplemented our diet with fresh produce. In turn, Mother sewed for Uncle Theodore's family and employees.

By the mid-1920s, prejudice against German-speaking minorities was escalating all over Czechoslovakia. Boycotts of German-owned stores and public harassment became commonplace. Instead of receiving a sought after promotion, Father lost his job—a terrible blow for him, as he had two children and a wife to support. Fortunately, some businessmen he had dealt with as a salesman cared more about his talents than his native tongue and tried their best to give him work. Even so, new opportunities came slowly. Every so often, he was hired to use his early training in graphic arts and drawing to create store displays in piece-good shops and to decorate the store windows of fashion and clothing stores. Sometimes Father brought home some of his work; the whole family helped cut out designs from poster boards, textured fabrics, and crepe paper at the large square kitchen table. Pens, glue, scissors, price tags and bottles of ink covered the table and kitchen counter. Although we children enjoyed helping Father and practicing our artistic skills, Mother was relieved whenever a project ended; for however brief a time, the kitchen was once again her domain.

Although Father enjoyed his creative work and took on as much as he could, his income was not enough to feed our family. In the early 1930s, when I was only six years old, Mother decided to open a fruit and vegetable stand a few blocks from our apartment building, about three miles from the city market. With her connections to the farmers in the area, including her brother, produce was easy to come by.

I remember her working from dawn until late at night. Every morning, except Sunday, she got up before daylight to purchase produce from the farmers on their way to the city market. Her brother was usually the first to drop off his bounty on his way to the market. Depending on the season, Mother would purchase crates of carrots, cauliflower, green beans, potatoes, and cabbage. Then she and Father would set up her stand, and by sunrise she would have a display of fresh fruits and vegetables ready for her customers. About twelve hours later, the stand had to be taken down and stored in the basement of our apartment building. Many evenings all of us brought in the stand on a small cart or carried the crates by hand. Six days a week we went through the same routine that took several hours. On some winter evenings, Mother came in after dark, her hands and face blue from the frigid weather. The small kerosene heater she used at her stand did not give her much relief from the bitter cold wind and neither did her earmuffs.

Once home, Mother's work was not over. Modern conveniences such as refrigerators, washing machines, dryers, and electric stoves were too expensive for us. We had a coal-burning stove with four burners. The kindling wood and coal for it had to be brought up from the basement. Mother must have been exhausted after a full day of work. I marvel now at how she always managed to have delicious food on the table: potatoes or bread, salads, and plenty of fresh, cooked vegetables. On special occasions we were treated to a piece of meat.

After the meal, Lilli and Erwin took turns cleaning and washing dishes but not without arguing about whose turn it was. Most of the time, I remained at the table with my plate in front of me. Mother insisted that we children clean our plates; food was not to be wasted. I turned up my nose to all cooked vegetables, carrots in particular—but Mother made no exceptions. I had to clean my plate; including carrots.

We lived in a small two-bedroom apartment on the ground floor of a three-story apartment building. Our side of the street was lined with apartments and on the other side were small one-story businesses and offices. Between our sidewalk and the roadway was a wide grassless area lined with tall shade trees where we children played hopscotch and marbles. We were not allowed to explore the back of the building, home to a lovely flower garden, but we all got to enjoy it because each apartment had a small balcony that overlooked the garden. Depending on the season, the fresh smell of lilacs, roses, or jasmine wafted through the balcony door into our apartment.

On our balcony, Father kept a large cabinet with tools of all kinds. He fixed just about anything that broke down, including the kitchen stove, furniture, a crystal operated radio, and the old Victrola. All the while he would hum or whistle. Mother kept her plants on that balcony. Once, I was allowed to stay up past my bedtime to see her night-blooming cactus open its beautiful white bloom. She had a special collection of them and was very excited for the two of us to witness something that happens in this plant's life once every ten years. Her favorite plants were geraniums and she had them in all colors. During the summer months, that balcony was my small little world where I loved to play. I did not have many toys, nor did I need many. A few small cardboard boxes, scraps of cloth, and a little doll or two kept me content for hours.

By the time I was seven, my brother Erwin looked after me. Whenever he wanted to go play with his friends, Mother made him take me along. I learned to play cowboys and Indians, cops and robbers, and all the other games boys played in those days. A few blocks down the street was a dairy distributor; its many ramps and storage bins were a perfect playground for the boys—and for me. I remember crying whenever I was unable to keep up with them. Though Erwin often fussed that he, rather than Lilli, was asked to watch over me, he was kind and inclusive. It was during those childhood games that Erwin and I formed the close bond that we enjoy to this day.

Erwin inherited this babysitting job from Uncle Hugo, my father's brother-in-law, who had owned a leather goods and furniture store in town. After his wife passed away, he could no longer manage his business by himself, so he came to live with us. He took me to and from kindergarten whenever he was well enough to walk. Uncle Hugo was a talented man, as was my father. The year before he died, he and Father built a dollhouse for me out of scraps. Everything was handmade—the furniture, drapes, carpeting and windows. It even had electricity and was the most beautiful thing I had ever seen. I treasured it for many years.

Uncle Hugo was dear to me for another reason. Every Sunday morning, he took me to his small, white stucco one-room church. He was not Catholic like my family. His tiny church was not as ornate and magnificent as ours, which was large and beautifully decorated—its high ceilings and stained glass windows lifted my eyes heavenward. His was a small, plain building with a crucifix over the altar and primitive, handmade pews that sat only a couple dozen people. I felt comfortable and safe in this simple space. Uncle Hugo taught me many things about God, and I was eager to learn more. On warm, sunny afternoons, I sat in his lap on the balcony and held onto his thin, callused hands while he read Bible stories to me for hours. When his eyes tired, he took off his glasses and continued where he had left off; the stories were in his heart.

My parents always said that I was a very inquisitive child, at times asking so many questions that they ran out of answers. But Uncle Hugo was a well of wisdom that never ran dry. He opened up a new world for me that satisfied my seven-year-old mind for knowledge about God. Even more important than answering all my questions, he taught me how to pray. At times, while listening to his prayers, I felt as if his words came straight from the depths of his soul. His expressions of humility and conviction provided a spiritual template for me.

Today I like to think that God gave me these formative years with my Uncle Hugo to prepare me not only for the trying times ahead but also for all that I would later learn about Him.

Before Uncle Hugo passed away, he gave me a small book he called his diary. Sitting on his lap on our favorite spot on the balcony, he said to me, "Whenever I face obstacles or difficulties in life, I write about them in my diary; then, whenever God sends me solutions, I record them. I have been blessed this way many times and I want you to have it. Promise me that whenever you will face disappointments or despair you will look in my diary for the comfort you need." Then he gave me a big hug and added, "I know you will find answers in it."

I promised. Not realizing then what an inspiration the diary would be in years to come, I placed the small black leather-bound book in my nightstand drawer.

Months later, just before Christmas 1937, he passed away. I knew I would miss him terribly that Christmas. My parents did too but somehow they managed, as they did every year, to make it a joyful, magical time. Every year on the twenty-third of December, Mother made Stollen, which we took to the bakery down the street because our oven was not large enough for the long, wide pastry. Lilli carried a loaf and Erwin and I followed behind carrying a second one. The baker put an identifying piece of paper on the fresh dough and told us when to pick up our pastries. We could hardly wait to pick up the warm and wonderful treat. As soon as we reached home, the smell of freshly baked goods permeated our home, filling it with holiday warmth and cheer. As soon as the Stollen was cool enough, Mother treated us to a cup of hot chocolate and the first piece of the pastry. As her cooking and baking was well known in the family, she liked to save some of it for company during the holidays. It wasn't until our guests came on Christmas Day that we would have another piece.

On Christmas Eve all stores closed at noon. Even Mother's vegetable stand was closed that day. In the afternoon, Lilli, Erwin and I would go sledding or ice skating and come home at dusk. When we walked through the front door, the living room was already closed to us children. While we ate and cleaned up, Father decorated the tree and arranged the gifts in the living room. Most of the Christmas presents were items we needed like clothing or shoes, but there was always a bowl of sweets with fruits and nuts. The tall fir tree was decorated with candy wrapped in colored tissue paper and other homemade decorations. It was the live candles on the tree, however, that gave the room that warm, festive look. While we tried on our new clothes, Father played Christmas carols on the Victrola and we sang along. When we were old enough, all of us went to Midnight Mass. Early the next morning I would quietly sneak up to the tree to pick my favorite piece of candy. Most Christmases Lilli and Erwin had already picked theirs but pretended to be sleeping so as not to spoil my fun. After all, I was the baby in the family.

One Christmas we received our first Telefunken radio. Knowing how much enjoyment it would bring to all of us, my parents had saved all year long for it. No longer did we have to constantly adjust the crystal to maintain reception, and oh, the music! The sound was simply beautiful. All of us were musically talented, but we did not have the financial means to pursue our talents. But we could sing! Whenever we were doing our chores, one of us would start singing a tune and the rest of us would spontaneously follow in harmony.

I have other fond memories of wintertime. At night, Father often told us stories, most of them very lighthearted and funny. Today I think that perhaps his imaginative and colorful description of ordinary stories is what made them so entertaining and special to us. His sense of humor carried him and all of us through many crises. Mother sometimes laughed so hard that tears rolled down her cheeks. She could laugh or cry on a moment's notice—something we often teased her about.

During these halcyon childhood days, the world was getting ready for war. Today I marvel at how well my parents protected us. When we weren't enjoying Father's stories, singing, or listening to music, Father listened intently to daily news broadcasts about political developments in our country and abroad. Whenever he wanted to be undisturbed, he sent us on an errand or found something for us children to do. However, by the end of 1938 we all knew it would not be long before there were some dramatic changes.

With the rise of Hitler in 1933, German nationalism among the dissatisfied German population of Czechoslovakia grew more widespread. The protection promised to the German minority by the League of Nations in 1918 was constantly violated and Hitler took the unrest to his advantage. Using the minorities' complaints as a pretext, he demanded the annexation of the highly industrialized area of the Sudetenland to Germany. To avoid war with Germany, Czechoslovakia's allies, Britain and France, signed the Munich Agreement, ceding the Sudetenland to the Third Reich. Father learned the news from a radio news broadcast and thought that the rest of the country would not be too far behind.

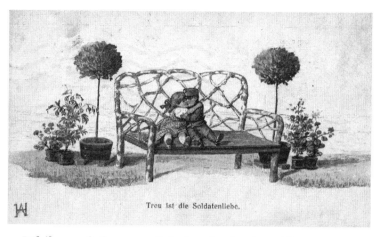

Treu ist die Soldatenliebe.

While my father was fighting during World War I, he sent my mother, whom he was courting at the time, this card. Its caption reads "True is the love of a soldier."

My parents on their wedding day, December 26, 1918

The Cathedral of St. Peter and Paul, a
beloved landmark in the city of Brno

The Storm Is Closing in

Barely six months later, on March 15, 1939, Father's predictions came true when Hitler's troops marched into and occupied Czechoslovakia. The Czechs put up no resistance; they had no army.

On that spring morning, Father heard the news anchor say, "Das ist der Volksdeutsche Sender Brünn" (This is the German Public Broadcasting Station in Brünn). Announcements were usually made in Czech and German, as everything in our lives was bilingual. This time, however, we heard only German. I looked at Father, not knowing what to make of this announcement. After all, he and Mother never discussed politics with us children. Father explained that German troops had just entered our homeland, making Czechoslovakia a protectorate of the Third Reich. I still did not comprehend the significance of the news but felt reassured when I saw his bright, hopeful eyes and heard him say, "Everything will change now. You'll see." After twelve years of short-lived part-time jobs, Father was ready for a new chapter.

Soon the radio announcer's voice was drowned out by the noise on the street. We looked out the window and saw German soldiers coming down the main street in tanks and trucks and on horseback, smiling and waving to the crowds that had gathered. The clatter and grinding noise of machinery against the cobblestones mixed with the onlookers' cheering and shouting were deafening.

Were these soldiers our liberators? Was the government they represented the solution to our problems, or would they bring additional ones? With no representation in the Czech government, ethnic Germans were ready for change. They did not know much about Hitler, only what the propaganda machine allowed them to hear. We were promised jobs, fair treatment, and better living conditions; we listened and believed.

A few days after Czechoslovakia was occupied and secured by the German military forces, we learned of Hitler's visit to the city. Father agreed to take me to see him. I remember standing by the Grand Hotel, not too far from the train station, waiting for his arrival. It was a damp, cloudy March day. After several hours, we heard the noise of automobile engines. First I saw a long line of trucks filled with troops. An entourage of Gestapo and SS uniformed guards followed, and finally the black, open limousine carrying Hitler appeared. He stood in the back seat, wearing a grey, wide lapel trench coat, his left hand holding on to his belt buckle and his right arm stretched out rigidly in his now infamous salutation. As the car drove by about thirty feet away from me, I could clearly see his solemn face staring into infinity. I wondered what he saw or thought. He did not look the way I imagined a liberator would. The crowds cheered and waved to him, but he did not move or wave back to them.

The scene blended into the grey, concrete buildings in the background and matched the gloominess of the chilly day. As I rubbed my hands to ward off the cold, I looked at Father. He did not utter a word. All I heard was a long sigh. Was it a sigh of relief or consternation? We stood there, long after the automobiles had passed, unable to dismiss what we had just seen. Years later, I recalled the image of this man who set out to conquer the world- a man who changed the lives of millions of people, including ours.

The changes that Father had envisioned came about six months later: he got back his old job with the textile firm. After his first month of work, he came up the stairs whistling and hugging my mother, who was standing at the top landing waiting for him. "Weist Du, Resl, das erste was wir tun werden ist eine grössere Wohnung finden" (You know, Resl, the first thing we're going to do is find a bigger apartment). Tears ran down Mother's cheeks. More than a decade of living in poverty, scrambling for odd jobs and working the vegetable stand were about to come to an end.

Our new third floor apartment was just around the corner. It had a large living room, a dining room with two big double paned windows, three bedrooms, an eat-in kitchen with a balcony, a hallway, and a big bathroom with an oversized tub.

I so looked forward to taking a bath in a regular bathtub. No longer would Father have to bring up the large washtub from the basement, and fill it with heated water from the stove. No longer would we have to take turns bathing in the kitchen on Saturday nights. There was no privacy and it took the whole evening for everyone to take a bath and put the kitchen back in order. With the move to a bigger apartment, we all looked forward to some much needed space.

The anxiety that came with moving items such as Mother's huge Madonna painting, a wedding present from her parents up the three flights of stairs was worth it—though it was hard to tell given how often Mother yelled out, "Vorsichtig," (be careful) to the movers as they navigated the long, narrow staircase. I also struggled maneuvering my own belongings—a birdcage, an aquarium with the two pet mice, and Ulli, my terrier—up the stairs. Given the view my pets and I would now have, I didn't mind at all. On the other side of the street were only single-story office buildings and stores, so I could stand at the living room window and see far above all the rooftops into the trees in the distance and to the river beyond. At night I gazed at the open, starry sky and watched the full moon play shadows on the rooftops below. My lookout was a perfect place for my imagination and dreams to take flight. I knew I was going to like our new home.

My parents had Lilli and I share a bedroom. It was their hope that we would grow closer to each other. Unfortunately, we did not. Ever since childhood, Lilli was "Vater's Liebling" (Daddy's favorite girl). Being the oldest came with certain privileges such as new clothes. I was the baby and was given Lilli's old clothes. "Hand-me-downs!" I cried as Mother tried convincing me that these clothes were as good as new. As Lilli entered her teen years, she wanted to wear more age-appropriate clothing. My parents bought her new, fashionable outfits—which to me reinforced that she was selfish and favored.

Jealousy fueled my resentment about how Lilli and I were treated differently. My performing in school recitals and plays, with the encouragement from my teachers to develop my talent, gave me a taste for stage performances—something I wanted to pursue as a career. Although Lilli and my parents knew that, they never attended any of my school performances. I did not get any encouragement at home to follow my dreams and when I begged Father to let me take voice lessons, he said,"You're still too young." However, when Lilli asked for singing and violin lessons, her charm and strong-willed personality prevailed. Quiet and unassuming, I swallowed my disappointment and did not ask again. I suspected that Lilli asked for the lessons as much to bait me as to pursue her interest in music. After all, she often spoke of becoming a teacher. Though she was not patient with me, she had a magical touch with a room full of young children.

Lilli followed both of her dreams. She entered teacher's college in 1941, continued taking singing lessons, and was accepted in the Brünn Opera House. Father was very proud of her. After all, she was the apple of his eye. I was jealous and hurt. Fueled by envy and a sense of personal defeat, I picked fights with her, mostly over insignificant things. Attuned to the cause of my frustration, she would belittle me and my talent. At times our arguments became so intense that Erwin had to intervene. When asked by my parents who had started the squabble, Lilli found a way to blame it all on Erwin.

I found solace in writing poetry and singing in my school's musical performances. My most avid supporters and confidants were also my best friends—Herta, who played the piano and Eva, who played the violin. Unlike with my sister, music brought us together rather than apart. We met at Herta's house to write lyrics to classical music and to try our hand at composing. We polished several pieces that we performed at school assemblies. Some of the skits we wrote and produced were quite funny, while others were based on history and less humorous in nature. Although these were amateur performances, we were proud of our accomplishments.

The all-girl elementary school we attended was a big, square three-story building. The east side was for Czech and the west for German students. The only area the two groups used— though never at the same time—was the courtyard in the middle of the building. Both schools taught basic German and Czech language courses as part of their daily curriculum. Our teachers and administrators were German; theirs were Czech. Other than casual meetings when school let out or during recess, we did not have much contact with the Czech students. We respected the boundaries of each other's domain.

When I entered fourth grade in the fall of 1939, only six months after Germany began occupying our country, we experienced changes my family did not expect or welcome. Swastika-studded signs and flags appeared on all government buildings. On German national holidays they were seen all over town along with Hitler's gigantic portrait.

Shortly after Germany's fateful invasion of Poland, the Nazis showed their true intentions: To "purify" our country as they had Germany. Newspapers were full of condemnation of Jews, blaming them for Germany's loss during World War I and for bringing economic ruin to the country. Vile and insidious caricatures of Jews appeared prominently with scathing captions in the daily newspapers. But the Nazis' pervasive and insidious propaganda was a very powerful tool of persuasion.

On the way home from school, I saw ugly graffiti all over town: store windows painted with the yellow stars of David and doors with "Jude" (Jew) written in big yellow letters. Posters and leaflets taped over other establishments read: "Die Juden sind unser Unglück" (The Jews are our misfortune). One day on my way home from school, I saw one of the Nazis' official automobiles in front of our neighborhood grocery store. I stopped just in time to see heavily armed SS men drag the owner, Mr. Hirsch, out from the back of the store and push him into the back seat of the automobile. As my neighbor stumbled toward the car, one of the guards used his club and kicked him, saying, "Ich helf Dir, Schwein" (I'll help you, pig). Mr. Hirsch must have just finished his noon prayer because his prayer shawl was still draped around his shoulders. I had known Mr. Hirsch for as long as I could remember; he had always been kind to me and my family. Whenever we had no money to pay for whatever groceries we needed, he'd "put it on our tab." Mother paid him whenever and how much she could. Now we were no longer allowed to patronize Jewish-owned stores. I was confused and angry but too afraid to ask any questions.

With the same year's early first snow, I saw a crowd of people gathered in front of our school watching a bonfire. German soldiers were burning books. Nazis had entered the school the night before and removed all texts that did not conform to their ideology. That morning we watched the pages of all those books blacken and crumble in the snow. The following day our school principal called the whole student body into the gymnasium and through a loudspeaker made the following announcement:

1. Members of the student body are not to have any friendly relations with Jews.

2. Jews are to sit apart from the rest of the class.

3. No German is to work with Jews on school assignments.

4. Jews are not allowed to participate in extracurricular activities.

Herta looked at me in disbelief. Our friend Eva was Jewish. Herta was a Protestant. I was Catholic. Our shared passion for music, poetry and literature had brought us together; now it looked as though our religion, which had never mattered to us, would tear us apart. As Herta and I looked around, we could not see her. Later we learned that she was not going to return and would be taught by a tutor. As we walked home that day, we looked up to her apartment window. She waved to us. We motioned for her to open the window so we could talk to her, but she did not. What would become of our friend?

Other questions haunted my young mind. If the Nazis wanted to purify the country, what were their plans for all the foreigners and Jews living here? Whenever I asked Father about the purification process, he explained that he and Mother had to meet certain requirements before they were deemed "acceptable" citizens. As long as they lived in the Austro-Hungarian Empire, only a certificate of residency was needed. However, when the Germans took over the country, Father chose to denounce his Austrian heritage to take on German citizenship to increase his chances of getting a job.

Had he sold his soul to the devil for his family's sake? Time would tell.

A few months later, when Herta and I were on the way home from school trying to catch Eva's daily waving a greeting to us, we did not see her behind the lace curtains; the apartment was empty.

A great sense of loss gripped me. This was the first time I saw freedom of choice taken away from someone who was close to me. I was frightened and angry.

I remembered what Uncle Hugo had written in his diary: "God is not only our Heavenly Father but also our best friend." Too distracted and upset to do my homework, too sad to sleep or eat—I turned to prayer, "Oh God, please help me understand the loss of my Jewish friend." Publicly I could not show my grief, but in my heart I could not let go of the pain. I wondered what other changes were ahead.

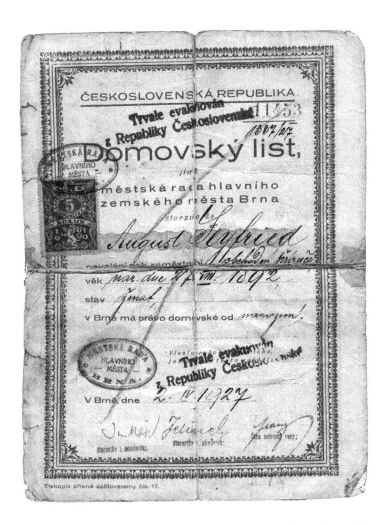

A certificate of residency in the Czechoslovakian Republic,
which was issued to my father on April 2, 1927.
It held very little significance to him or to anyone
else after Hitler occupied his homeland.

In hopes of improving his chances for employment
after twelve years without full-time work, Father chose
to apply for a German certificate of citizenship.

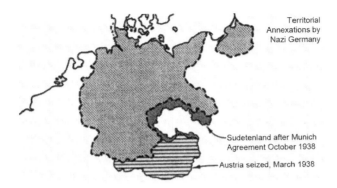

The Sudetenland after the Munich
Agreement in October 1938[3]

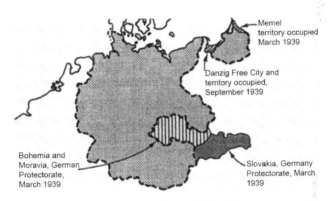

Bohemia, Moravia, and the German
Protectorate in March 1939[4]

3   Dornberg, John. "Germany's Expellees and Border Changes." German Life:
    Anniversary Issue July 1995: 21. Print.

4   Ibid.

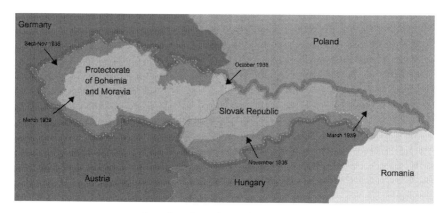

Czechoslovakia after 1939[5]

5 "Czechoslovakia 1939" by derivative work: ThemightyquillFirst_ Czechoslovak_Republic.SVG: *derivative work: ThemightyquillCzechoslovakia01.png: ElectionworldBlank_map_of_ Europe_-_Atelier_graphique_colors.svg: historicairImage:Rzeczpospolita 1939.svg: HalibuttImage:GDR.png: Kgberger16:36, 13 September 2007 (UTC) - First_Czechoslovak_Republic.SVGImage:GDR.png. Licensed under CC BY-SA 3.0 via Wikimedia Commons - http://commons. wikimedia.org/wiki/File:Czechoslovakia_1939.SVG#mediaviewer/ File:Czechoslovakia_1939.SVG

CHAPTER THREE

Reinhard Heydrich

ONE OF THE FIRST CHANGES was Hitler's sending Reinhard Heydrich, a high-ranking SS officer and head of the Gestapo to control the Protectorate. He was known for his iron fist policies and his ruthless implementation of them. All foreign publications and films were banned. The Ministry of Enlightenment made sure that nothing could be seen or read that was defamatory or damaging to the image of Nazi Germany. Our cultural diet was determined accordingly. Concert halls were restricted to offering music of Nazi-approved composers only. Initially this included only Germans and Austrians; later they added Italian and certain composers from neutral countries.

Hitler's idea was that if he gave people certain information often enough, they would eventually come to believe it, virtually eliminating any opposition to the Third Reich. His measures were pervasive and extreme. All radios had to be turned in for "adjustments," which involved disabling reception to foreign transmitters. Those who did not comply and were caught listening on "illegal" frequencies, were arrested and subsequently punished. In school we no longer opened with prayer. Instead, we stood in silent attention while the public address system blared the German national anthem; we had to learn and memorize the lyrics.

Teachers who were deemed suitable by the new regime came to our school as replacements for the mentors whom we had grown to love. We studied from new history textbooks. Any historical account that portrayed Germany in a negative light was lifted or altered. Children were not taught history: they were force-fed propaganda. The Ministry's brainwashing and propaganda did not stop there. Our "cultural enrichment" began with films that promoted the greatness of Hitler and the condemnation of Jews. Gradually, we saw politically neutral films and stage productions. In fact, Brunn became the first testing ground in the new Protectorate for German and Austrian opera, drama, and symphony orchestra companies. Free tickets were given to schools as part of our cultural enrichment. At age eleven, I saw Puccini's *Madam Butterfly* and Wagner's *Tannhäuser*. At first, opera made me sleepy because I could not follow the storyline, but once I learned to read about the upcoming productions, I enjoyed going to the theatre and opera became my favorite.

For over three years, until the end of the war, I had the opportunity to see many famous operas, operettas, dramas, and plays. Arias from Verdi's *Aida* and duets from Strauss' Operetta *Die Fledermaus* still take me back to those red velvet seats in the Brünn Opera House. These enriching cultural events were meant to "balance" or "soften" the Nazis' otherwise harsh and ruthless propaganda, which was in full force by 1942. "One people, one country, one leader" was the war cry throughout the country. There had to be "Gleichschaltung" (complete conformity and unity). What some people did not realize was the price of this conformity: mental and physical enslavement. For fear of being scrutinized and watched, some people lived in silence and looked the other way, never challenging the government's statement on anything. They knew that an arrest for only minor infractions or the slightest criticism of the Reich could lead to harsh treatment during interrogations, imprisonment, and even death.

In the summer of 1942 we heard of the assassination of Reinhard Heydrich. Furious over losing him, Hitler avenged Heydrich's death by ordering the village of Lidice and Ležáky, about ten miles outside of Prague, to be wiped from the face of the earth. The day following the assassination, the men from the villages, 1300 hundred of them, were lined up at the market square and shot.

Their wives and children were sent off to concentration camps. The villages were then leveled, houses burned and fields dug up until there was no trace left of the villages. The Czechs were outraged and the hatred for all Germans intensified.

During this time of uncertainty and unrest, Father announced that he would be leaving his job to work as a translator. His decision came as a surprise because he seemed to enjoy his work. His only explanation was that the German police were paying high wages for translators and that his fluency in Czech made his skills especially marketable. Not knowing what his new job entailed, I thought that it was a perfect public relations job for his ready wit and easy-going personality.

He had often told us funny World War I stories about his interactions with other soldiers, so I looked forward to hearing some new entertaining yarns, but they never came. Instead, Father became more and more lost in his own thoughts. As time went by, he no longer whistled his favorite tunes while tinkering on the balcony and no longer found the time to entertain us in the evenings before bedtime. I could tell that something was bothering him. When I asked about his job, he indicated that it was classified. I knew that meant he was obligated not to talk about it. I never asked again. Only after the war did Father tell me the truth.

As the war escalated, so did Nazi propaganda. By 1942, Germany had seized most of Europe in their quest for "Lebensraum" (living space). The Russian military battle lines spanned over three thousand miles and Germany did not have the necessary troops to secure that distance. Men between the ages of sixteen and sixty were being drafted. Women who served in the Reichsarbeitsdienst (RAD for short), a mandatory labor force for women, replaced men on farms, in factories, and even in military non-combat units.

One day Lilli was called to report to the RAD for training, about fifty kilometers north of Brünn to a large camp near Olomouc in Moravia. It was the first time one of us had to leave home for an extended period of time, but we were not surprised because this service was mandatory for all young women. "We can go see her after basic training," Mother said, trying to reassure us. Lilli packed her bags and cleared out her part of our room. I wondered whether I would enjoy having a quiet bedroom all to myself. Though I wouldn't miss our arguments, I did not want her to go.

Not long after Lilli left, Erwin was drafted into the infantry, a far more unpredictable and dangerous call than a labor corps. It caught all of us by surprise because he had not yet turned eighteen. I wanted to help prepare him for the long marches, so just before his departure I taught him how to mend socks to help keep his feet from blistering. Shortly after he left, I received a thank you letter in which he asked me to send him more yarn, because he was teaching his fellow soldiers his newly acquired skill.

Seeing his two oldest children in uniform was Father's proudest moment; they had grown up. But Mother thought they were both too young, particularly Erwin, who looked so thin and boyish in his grey, military garb.

By the end of 1942, troop losses were extremely high on both sides. Reluctantly the German press reported the loss of Stalingrad. Hitler decreed three days of mourning for the troops lost there; theaters and restaurants were closed and sports events were banned for the rest of the war. For the first time since the war had begun, we heard news of German forces retreating, a sign of a turning point on the Russian front. Mother was worried about Erwin's getting too close to the battle lines. From one of his letters we learned that he was somewhere in eastern Hungary—precariously close to the heat of the conflict.

At home, civil defense authorities were preparing the public for eventual air attacks. In compliance with governmental orders, everyone, including business owners, observed blackouts between dusk and dawn. Not complying with these regulations would result in an arrest and a charge of treason. Though we cooperated, I did not understand what all the fuss was about. All I knew was that at night the city reminded me of a ghost town.

The few street lights that lit my way home after a late night concert used reflector shields, making the light beams softer and lower. Lights in our apartment were turned on only when necessary and the blackout shades were drawn at dusk.

"You're going to ruin your eyes," Mother would tell me when I read thick novels in bed by flashlight. I read this way, hoping she would not notice how long I stayed up, but she usually did. How could I resist reading just one more chapter in a suspenseful novel like *The Count of Monte Cristo*?

It did not take long for me to learn the reason for the blackouts. Though we heard air raid sirens once or twice a week late at night, no one paid attention to them since we heard only the warning sounds, which were given whenever radar detected enemy planes. During those nightly "fire drills" as I called them, I wondered how we would distinguish between German and enemy planes. I learned that lesson soon enough.

As the battle lines on the ground moved closer to Germany, so did the activities in the skies. By the end of 1943, we could set our clocks by the sirens. Enemy planes were now being dispatched during the day from former Italian air bases, which were now occupied by British and American forces, just a short distance away. There was never enough time for warnings to be given. At 11:00 a.m. every day, almost to the minute, the wailing sound of the sirens resonated all over the city, telling us that enemy planes approaching the city had been sighted by radar. Instantaneously everyone would run to the closest underground shelter and all traffic would come to a standstill.

Soon the streets were deserted; the city seemed to be holding its breath. Seven days a week, combat formations of heavy enemy bombers flew high above the city on their way to their targets, painting the sky with streaks of contrails. On overcast days or at night we did not see them, but we learned to discern their engines' distinct sound. We learned to judge the height the formation was flying: the higher they flew, the less chance there was that we would be the next target. The frightening thought was always there: When will it be our turn?

Mahen Theatre in the city of Brno, where I spent many
memorable evenings during my middle school years[6]

All family members had their picture taken on Christmas
1943, the last holiday we spent together as a family.

6   Börkur Sigurbjörnsson available under Creative Commons attribution
    license

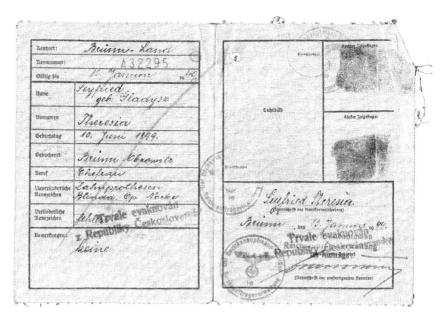

This German identification card was issued to my
mother in 1944. After the war, such a card was of
no help because she was an ethnic German.

CHAPTER FOUR

A City in Ruins

OUR FIRST ATTACK came in the summer of 1944. I was walking through the narrow, cobblestone streets in the old part of the city on my way home from shopping when the sirens went off. Knowing that the sirens would be sounding off around 11:00 a.m., I should have taken Mother's advice earlier that morning and planned my errands for the afternoon, but I didn't. It was Saturday and the streets and nearby markets were crowded with shoppers. From the siren's sound I could tell that enemy planes were approaching the city; this was not a warning. Too far from home to seek shelter there, I hurried down Orli Street towards the catacombs of one of the oldest churches in the city and started down the stairway. The narrow, steep pathway leading to the underground passageways was crowded with people pushing each other in a nervous panic.

When I finally reached the lowest level, the wooden benches that lined the walls were full. Civil Defense had designated many public buildings throughout the city as public bomb shelters. In the downtown area there were hundreds of them clearly marked on the outside of each building and equipped with fire extinguishers, gas masks, shovels, picks, and first aid supplies. Depending on the shelter's size, benches were also provided.

As I sat down, I looked around me. I was among about one hundred people—all of us quiet, listening for noises from above. The slight rumblings sounded like an approaching thunderstorm; we were too far down to hear more than that. After about an hour, officials announced that the raid was over and we could start coming up. The deafening sirens that signaled it was safe to leave had not penetrated the thick walls of the old Roman structure. Once the first few people reached ground level, panic erupted. The street was covered with rubble and shattered glass; the building across the street was just a shell. In the middle of the roadway was a large crater. The watchmaker's clock down the street had stopped at 12:01 p.m. Dust from the falling debris still filled the air. As I made my way through the rubble of glass and bricks, the thought occurred to me that I could have been buried alive. Terrified, I hurried to get home. From a distance, I could see our house still standing. Mother, with tears in her eyes, stood outside waiting for me. "Thank God you're all right," she cried as I ran towards her.

One Sunday afternoon a week or two later, I sat in the living room between the two eastern windows where the hot summer sun could not reach me, sewing a button on to my blouse. All of a sudden I heard the *tat-tat-tat-tat* sound of a machine gun outside the window, and instinctively I ducked. Window glass flew all around me; the next second it was over. I ran out the front door and down the stairs. Mother was right behind me. "Are you hurt?" she called out to me. As we rushed to the cellar, I assured her I was okay. A low flying fighter plane had whizzed over the house and randomly shot at our building. "There were no sirens," I heard someone behind me say. Within a few minutes all of the tenants had arrived. Everyone was very confused; some showed signs of having been awakened from a Sunday afternoon nap. While we were in panic over the lone fighter plane shooting at our building, a squadron of bombers had approached the city and before the sirens could sound off, we heard the first bombs detonate close by. There was no anti-aircraft artillery, no civil defense warnings. The enemy had caught everyone by surprise. We rushed to take our seats in the basement.

"Frau Hoffman and the baby," I cried out, remembering our neighbor who was not among those in the cellar. I had visited her just hours before. By the basement door stood a German soldier, a passerby who had sought shelter in our basement. "Come with me," I asked him as I started up the stairs. "There is a lady with her baby still upstairs." Mother tried to hold me back but the urgency in my voice made her relent. Heavy smoke came through the broken windows of the staircase as we climbed up the stairs. A few hundred yards away, in the back of our apartment building, was a lumberyard that had received a direct hit. A brisk wind blew the smoke in our direction. I paused, wondering whether we could reach our neighbor before we had to turn back; it was getting difficult to breathe.

There was no response when the soldier knocked on the door. Realizing the dangerous situation we were in, the soldier broke down the door. The apartment was already full of smoke and I could barely find my way. We crawled to the kitchen, where I had last seen Frau Hoffman. She was sitting on the floor with her infant in her arms, unconscious. To safeguard against the smoke, we threw some wet towels from a nearby linen basket over them and ourselves. We made our way down the three flights of stairs—the soldier carrying Frau Hoffman and I holding her baby. The soldier and I both coughed and tried to catch pockets of clean air. On the last landing, just before the basement door, I fainted. Later I learned that some of the tenants who were in the basement came to our assistance. After I came to, I asked Mother about the soldier, she told me that before she could speak to him, he was gone. I wished I'd had the opportunity to thank him.

We started seeing fewer and fewer troops on the streets. German battle lines on the Eastern Front moved closer to our homeland as the scattered armies slowly but steadily retreated. German defenses weakened with each air raid and bombing—so much so that anti-aircraft artillery was no longer employed. Allied bombers had complete control of the skies.

On November 20, 1944, there were no sirens when the bombs started falling. As soon as we heard their whistling sound as they poured out of the sky, we hurried to our assigned space in the basement. The first close explosion detonated before we could sit down.

The building shook vigorously but did not collapse. The vibrations loosened the plaster ceiling, covering us with white dust. Through the cracks in the door on the backside of the basement I could see flashes of fire against the black, smoke-covered sky. There were several detonations in the distance and then there was silence; no one moved. Sirens did not call off the raid. Soon the bombing started again. The enemy bombers were demolishing the city. We stayed in the shelter for a while longer. When there was neither a siren calling off the raid nor any more explosions, we slowly filed out of the shelters and onto the street. The devastation was enormous. Every building on our street was either totally demolished or severely damaged, filling the roadway with mountains of bricks and rubble. Windows were blown out in the few buildings that remained standing; glass covered the sidewalks.

One of the officials surveying the scene from his patrol car told us of damage in several other neighborhoods. As he left, he shouted the general direction of the worst devastation. Our first concern was for Aunt Rosa, a great aunt on father's side of the family, who lived about three miles from our house, on the west side of the city—the general direction given by the driver.

Mother and I ran off to find her. We had to navigate around the areas cordoned off because of debris, craters, and unexploded bombs. A few incendiary bombs lit several buildings. Heavy smoke covered the city, making it difficult to breathe. Some of the landmarks in the city were damaged; others were reduced to shells, their contents piled high in the center. Our church down the street had lost its steeple and part of the front entrance; stores that once housed merchandise had been annihilated. Our school, however, was unscathed; only the windowpanes in all the buildings surrounding it, were gone. Saint Peter's Cathedral on the hill overlooking the city was still standing—though it had lost some shingles and stained glass windows. Wrapped up in their own wires and blocked by craters, the deserted streetcars could not move.

As we made our way to Aunt Rosa's apartment building, my heart beat faster and faster. We could not see the upper floors and rooftop of her house, which had always been visible from a distance. As we came around the corner of her street, we found a terrifying sight: the front wall of the building was gone. Some empty window frames hung loosely attached to the building and others were gone completely. I saw rooms with furniture and wardrobes full of clothes, dusty and filled with debris. Doors were ajar, just as they had been before the tenants left their apartments to hide in the shelter. The building looked like an open doll house. The piles of brick made the street almost impassable. As we came closer, we saw civil defense personnel helping someone lying on the ground. "Oh no," Mother cried out, "It is Rosa." We hurried to her side. One of the rescuers told us that they had to get her down by ladder from the third floor.

Aunt Rosa never liked going to the bomb shelter; she always thought it was a waste of time because she had "more important things to do." She later told us that when she heard the bombs fall, she decided to go to the shelter after all. Halfway out the door, she remembered to get her keys from the kitchen cabinet. It was that decision that had saved her life. As she stood by the cabinet, a bomb hit the building and everything behind her caved in. The force of the explosion threw her into the only standing corner on that floor of the building. Smoke and dust were so thick she could not see. In shock, she stood frozen in that corner until help arrived hours later.

After a few days of medical care in the hospital, Aunt Rosa came to live with us. Although her physical injuries healed quickly, putting her life back together was not going to be so easy. The trauma of her experience would likely leave emotional scars forever. She was a forty-five-year-old widow whose only son was serving in the German Air Force. We knew that it would take some time for her to gain back the strength needed for when he returned home. Mother replaced some of the material necessities she had lost. Mementoes and treasured keepsakes were gone. Memories were all that she had left.

Though Christmas was only a few weeks away, we were not looking forward to it. Shortly before the holidays, Cousin Bedřich, with his wife and baby, came looking for shelter. Fearing Russian capture, they had fled Eastern Europe ahead of the retreating German Army. We spent half of our time living in the bomb shelter and the other half in our apartment—all the while listening for airplanes as we tended to necessities like washing clothes, bathing and cooking. Bedřich's family came with only their bare essentials. Provisions were already short; stores had difficulty getting staple items and refugees were not entitled to ration coupons. But Mother would not hear of sending them to the public emergency shelters or soup kitchens. While they stayed with us, Mother used her canned vegetables and fruits, for which she had so carefully bartered for at the farms the summer before, and stored in the pantry. By the time our relatives left, our pantry shelves were bare. When Mother saw me looking at the empty pantry, she said, "If you share in time of others' needs, God will provide in time of yours." I later learned she was right.

CHAPTER FIVE

An Unwanted Child

ON DECEMBER 24, 1944, we received bad news: neither Lilli nor Erwin could get leave that year for Christmas. A few days earlier, Mother had told me that Father was not going to be with us for the holidays because he was temporarily assigned to another city. She had tears in her eyes when she added, "Pray for him." I did not understand her special request as I always included the family in my prayers, but I did not ask for an explanation. Only after the war ended did I learn of his true whereabouts that Christmas, and the reason for his absence.

I had such wonderful memories of the holidays the year before, when the whole family had enjoyed a traditional dinner together. Although some supplies were rationed and difficult to obtain, Mother had managed to get some flour for the traditional Stollen, fresh vegetables, and a large goose from her brother Theodore in the country, which she roasted for the occasion. For the following day, December 26, my parents had invited extended family for their twenty-fifth wedding anniversary. We laughed and enjoyed the wonderful food Mother had prepared. Not surprisingly, everyone who was invited, came. After all, Mother's dumplings were the best in the family. The following day we had our pictures taken for the occasion at a nearby studio, not realizing that those were to be the last ones taken of us together as a family.

One year later, with Father, Lilli and Erwin still gone, Mother showed tremendous strength. She tended to our guests' needs and whenever I complained about something, she reminded me "Be grateful. You still have a home. Others don't have that."

The traditional tree with its warm and festive candlelight was missing that year as was the aroma of freshly baked Stollen. Mother was able to get some fresh vegetables and flour from the country and prepared a plain but delicious dinner, consisting of dumplings and gravy, kale, salads, and beets. The traditional roasted goose was missing that year as well, but we were grateful for what we did have. For dessert we had gingerbread cookies, this time made without the usual ingredients and spices, but a treat nevertheless. Mother broke from tradition and custom and offered a prayer, not the usual one from the book of prayers, but one coming from her heart. She thanked God for those sharing the meal with us and asked for both a blessing on the food and protection for our family in harm's way. At the end, she prayed for our own safety in the days ahead. It was a quiet holiday. Even the enemy respected the sanctity of that day; there were no sirens on Christmas Day.

By mid-January of 1945, Aunt Rosa had found more suitable housing with a relative in the country, and Cousin Bedřich and his family left in hopes of reaching Prague before the trains stopped operating. As we parted, our prayers went with them, knowing that only God could protect them until they reached their destinations.

Our railroad station was overflowing with refugees who were fleeing the advancing Allied Forces. The few trains still operating were dangerously overloaded. People hung onto the trains heading for the interior of the country; some even were perched on the cars' rooftops. There were passengers who never reached their destinations; trains were a favorite target for enemy planes.

Allied Forces from the west were making their final thrust into Germany. From the east, the Russian armies began closing in. Allied bombers stepped up their attacks. In destroying such strategic targets as railroad stations, they also demolished block after block of buildings.

By March 1945, the end of the war was in sight; however, the course it would take was not clear. We faced not only fighting military forces but also our Czech neighbors. Six years of German occupation revived the old political feud and hatred toward Germany that had existed for centuries. We were certain that native, ethnic Germans would be prime targets. Although our family had good relations with our Czech neighbors, we still did not know what to expect.

Several months before, my parents had talked and made arrangements with friends and family in case an emergency occurred. In March, Mother let everyone know where she and I would go in case we needed to evacuate. Family friends, Mr. and Mrs. Peterka, who lived in nearby Modřice, invited us to stay with them if it became necessary. Relieved, Mother accepted their invitation.

Our list of family contacts and friends in our area included Uncle Theodore, who lived with his family on his farm in the country. Aunt Mina, my father's sister-in-law, decided to leave the city when evacuation was warranted and stay with other relatives in nearby Bohunice. Our family friend, Steffi Jurka, a widow, was going to stay in her apartment in the city. She had no other place to go but declined to come with us.

Life became strangely normal in its abnormality. We learned to live from one day to the next. Newspapers stopped publishing, radio stations ceased broadcasting, and telephone service was cut off. Streets became more and more deserted in broad daylight. We no longer heard the familiar sounds of factory whistles, cars, or church bells. Schools and stores were closed and an 8:00 p.m. curfew was enforced. We spent most of our time searching for depleted daily necessities and basic food items. Money became worthless; everything was bartered. Mother exchanged a set of silver candleholders, which one of our neighbors admired and wanted, for two bars of soap. A bag of noodles changed hands for a pair of shoes.

By early April, we received news and messages by word of mouth only. One day we learned that the Germans would defend our city, only to hear the following morning that it was declared an "open city," which meant the Germans would surrender it to the Russians. German fighting units had left our area some time ago; only straggling, small groups of retreating infantry men were occasionally seen on the street hurrying westward. We were in no man's land.

The prospect of the Russian Army occupying our city frightened us because we had heard about their thievery, rapes, and murders. There was nothing that we could do to prepare or protect ourselves ahead of time. Nothing.

People with handcarts or loaded down bicycles struggled to get away. Soon the streets were empty. By mid-April, Mother decided it was time for us to leave the city to stay with Mr. and Mrs. Peterka. Late one night, Mother and I went to our section of the basement, where we kept firewood, coal, and other supplies. Months before, during the heavy air raids, Father had dug a hole into the basement floor. In it he placed a strong metal box with essential documents and other memorabilia. In case of a fire, these items would be safe.

Mother and I retrieved the box that contained ID cards, diplomas, and photographs, as well as birth, marriage, and death certificates. Mother had to decide what we would need for survival and what had only sentimental value. There, in the dark hole lay a lifetime worth of memories, things we may never see again. She looked at some of the pictures and keepsakes one more time and in a small pouch she placed documents and some pictures she was going to take with her. The rest she put ever so gently back into the metal box, which she covered with dirt.

Still and quiet, we sat on the old chairs in the dark basement by candlelight. Though Mother tried to conceal her worries from me, I could see that she was troubled. I knew that my words would not console her. When I reached for her hand, she gently touched mine. I heard her long sigh and saw tears roll down her cheeks. We sat there, holding hands until the candle burned out.

Early the next morning we packed our belongings in a small handcart. Before leaving, we both walked through the apartment one last time. Mother turned to me and said, "This was a happy home for me." I cried and said goodbye to my favorite place at the living room window, the spot where I had written poetry and composed lyrics. I looked once more over the rooftops of the city, opened the windows and my bird's cage, and my winged pet flew away. I also released my two white mice. Uli, the fox terrier, came with us. As we left the apartment, I remembered Uncle Hugo's diary and turned around to retrieve it from the secret drawer in my room.

It was unusually quiet as we walked through the streets and outskirts of the city and along the country road towards Modřice, a small village about five miles south of the city. There was no traffic in either direction. Most of the city's population had evacuated earlier to escape the possible house-to-house fighting between the advancing Russian Army and existing pockets of German infantry. At one point we passed a cluster of young German soldiers walking in the opposite direction without weapons. Two were injured. If there had ever been any drive in them to fight, there certainly was none left. They looked battered and hungry. We had no food to share with them, so we passed them quickly and averted our eyes.

I was glad when we reached our destination, the Peterka's home, which was one of a dozen along the main highway into the village. About fifty feet behind the house, high on an embankment running parallel to the highway, were the railroad tracks of the main line going to and from Vienna. Across the road were acres upon acres of freshly planted fields, untouched by bombings. The air was fresh and clean; it smelled like spring.

Mr. and Mrs. Peterka and their eighteen-year-old daughter Anna greeted us warmly. Mr. Peterka helped unloading our cart as Mrs. Peterka, a heavyset lady with deep brown eyes, came towards mother and, with a ready smile and a big hug, said to her, "Welcome to both of you, I hope you will feel safe in our home." She was German and her husband was Czech. Just as with my parents, their difference in heritage did not affect their relationship. Mr. Peterka was slender and short with thinning hair and a ruddy complexion. Years of working in the fields showed in his callused hands. Before retirement he worked as a foreman on Uncle Theodore's farm and stopped by our house often, unloading produce before proceeding to the city market. Our families' friendship continued long after Mother closed down the vegetable stand and Mr. Peterka stopped working. Anna, their daughter, had her mother's beautiful brown hair and eyes. After the war, she wanted to resume her studies in Brünn to become a veterinarian.

After we had something to eat, Mr. Peterka showed us the property. As we stood in their front yard, he pointed to the basement. "There is a bunker below. Come, I will show you." When we reached the basement, we noticed a chute leading from one of the small windows to the basement floor—a handy device for unloading coal or large quantities of produce. He lifted the chute; behind it was a small door going through the foundation of the house. As he opened it, he explained that it took him eighteen months to build his "bomb shelter," as he called it. He had dug a narrow tunnel, which we climbed into by stepping down a ten-foot ladder. We then entered a small passageway that led to an 8 by 10 foot room. Pipes leading from that room in several directions to the surface of the front yard of the house provided fresh air. The pipes were undetectable from the outside. This bunker was a perfect hiding place.

On April 20, one day before my fifteenth birthday and three days after our arrival, Mrs. Peterka asked her daughter to go and buy some fresh milk from one of the farmers a couple of miles down the road and to take me along. On our way back, we took a footpath along the back walls of several large barns, each of us carrying a jug of milk. Suddenly we heard some low flying enemy planes closing in on us. Anna called out for me to hurry. Our hearts pounding and legs unsteady, we ran to a large cement pipe that ran through a nearby ditch, found an opening and crawled into the dark space. Within seconds we saw several German Messerschmitts and foreign planes creating quite a scramble above us. Bullets flew all around us. Yelling above the noise, Anna told me she had heard rumors of the Germans hiding tanks in the barns that we had just passed. The retreating German forces must have forgotten to destroy them, but now they had returned to defend their weapons and equipment. The enemy planes were unsuccessful in destroying the barns or tanks inside, and the only success the German planes had was to disperse the Allies' attempt. Soon the road was quiet again and we were able to continue walking home. Though still shaken up from the incident, when we arrived home, Anna had to recall for her parents every detail of our frightening experience. We were glad to be safely home.

The next morning promised to be a beautiful spring day. Peaceful and unmarked by any trace of battle, the sky was a brilliant, sun-washed blue. Everything was quiet on the road; only an occasional rooster could be heard making its wake-up call. As we were enjoying my birthday breakfast, I heard the all too familiar sound of plane engines. I looked out the window and saw a tight formation of enemy bombers slowly flying over the house. I ran out the back door to get a closer look when another wave appeared on the horizon, then another right behind it, and on and on until the sky was full of them. They flew so low I could see every detail—their numbers and colorful markings and even some of the pilots' faces.

The noise was deafening. Anna and I crawled up the embankment in back of the house to see where they were heading. When the planes reached our city, the formation broke up; they had reached their target.

Hundreds of bombs dropped from the planes and onto the city below; we could not count the explosions fast enough. Although I was glad not to be there to experience it, I was thinking of those who were. As I reached for Anna's hand, she trembled and hugged me. I asked the Lord to save Father from possible danger if indeed he was in the city. I had not seen him since December of 1944, when our family spent Christmas without him. I was told that he was temporarily assigned to another city. I hoped that he was safe.

Hours after the attack, the dust and smoke on the horizon cleared. We figured that this bombing was to clear the way for the Russian infantry. That night, we heard enemy planes flying over but did not hear any bombs detonate. Mr. Peterka went outside to investigate. He returned with a handful of papers, explaining, "They've dropped some leaflets written in German and Russian, asking the German fighting forces to surrender and granting them safe passage." He suggested we go to bed fully dressed just in case we had to be mobile in a hurry. Mother and I made our bed on a large mattress in the basement. Neither one of us could sleep. At about 4:00 a.m.—not yet dawn—we heard an ear-piercing noise that shook the foundation of the house. We could hear dishes and books flying off the shelves and furniture sliding across the floor. Mother and I jumped up and ran upstairs. Mr. Peterka told us that the Russians had moved a battery of eight portable rocket launchers into the fields across the road. "I heard they had a new weapon, the Katyushka, which is capable of firing sixteen rockets at one time," he explained. "They are clearing the way for the infantry. I am afraid they will be here by morning. Try to get some rest," he suggested. "We will need our strength. I will let you know if anything happens."

Mother and I lay there on our mattress. "Margit, I have some-thing to tell you and I hope that you will understand. I don't want you to interrupt me. Otherwise I cannot finish." Her voice was strained. She was close to tears. Not saying a word, I nodded my head. "Everything looks so hopeless," she continued. "I don't know how much more I can take." After a few minutes, as if searching for the right words, she proceeded to tell me of the pain and sense of loss she and Father felt during their first few years of marriage, losing their first baby girl, Margita. Her voice broke down. "After Erwin was born and Father had lost his job, we did not plan to have another child; so, when I was pregnant with you, it came as a sur-prise." She was searching for the right words. Was she trying to tell me that I was an unwanted child? "Margit," she paused for another moment, then slowly continued, "We could not afford another child. Perhaps it was God's will for you to take Margita's place in our lives, I don't know. But now," she was fighting with emotions, "Forgive me, Margit, and may the Lord forgive me also, if I did not have you by my side, I would consider taking my life. I could not go on." I was fighting back my tears, afraid to say anything. We both were struggling with our feelings. Mother started to cry. I thought of Uncle Hugo's diary, but it was out of reach. Oh, how I needed his love and words of wisdom right now!

I finally broke down, put my arms around her, and cried bitter tears. I could now explain and release the pain I had felt over the years. No wonder I had so often felt unloved and not part of my family—like a stepchild. Now that our lives were in danger, I had finally learned the truth and felt desperate to consider what it meant. But this was not the time for introspection; we needed to concentrate on surviving. Mother interrupted my thoughts.

"Something else you need to know," she slowly continued after a long pause. "Since we don't know what is going to happen to us and we might get separated, you need to know that in my little pouch of papers there is a list of names and addresses. Safeguard and memorize that list." I had to interrupt her. I did not understand. "Last Christmas," she explained, "when you were told that your father was out of town, he was really being held for interrogations. The Germans suspected him of collaborating with the enemy and arrested him as politically unreliable. I looked at her, refusing to believe what I had just heard. "What did he do?" I asked.

"In his work, most of the translations between Czechs or Jews and the German gendarmes were done during interrogations of political prisoners. Your Father knew what the Germans did with prisoners who were found guilty, and he did all he could to help the detainees. Sometimes, when translating, he altered their answers if he felt they were too incriminating. Other times he supplied the prisoners with food and messages from home. This is the list of people your Father helped. Now that the war is almost over, I can finally tell you the truth." Mother continued telling me of incidents Father had confided in her about his work that she could not talk about then. "You understand, don't you?" Her voice trembled as she handed me the list.

I could not answer. I was stunned.

I now understood the change in Father's personality after he started working for the Germans. That was when my parents realized the true nature of Nazi Germany and could not talk about it. I closed my eyes and thanked God they had not been sucked up into the bottomless vacuum of the Nazis' lies and propaganda. By helping others, however small the gesture, they had chosen their beliefs over mental enslavement. "Thank you, God!" I thought, "But where is Father?"

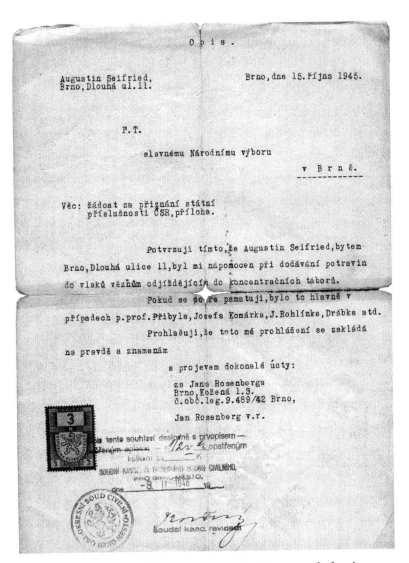

O p i s .

Augustin Seifried,   Brno,dne 15.října 1945.
Brno,Dlouhá ul.11.

P. T.

slavnému Národnímu výboru

v B r n ě.

Věc: žádost za přiznání státní
     příslušnosti ČSR,příloha.

        Potvrzuji tímto,že Augustin Seifried,bytem

Brno,Dlouhá ulice 11,byl mi nápomocen při dodávání potravin

do vlaků vězňům odjíždějícím do koncentračních táborů.

        Pokud se dobře pamatuji,bylo to hlavně v

případech p.prof.Přibyla,Josefa Komárka,J.Rohlínka,Drábka atd.

        Prohlašuji,že toto mé prohlášení se zakládá

na pravdě a znamenám

                s projevem dokonalé úcty:

                za Jana Rosenberga
                Brno,Kožená 1.3.
                č.obč.leg.9.489/42 Brno,

                Jan Rosenberg v.r.

One of many affidavits acknowledging my father's
assistance to detainees in Nazi custody. His help kept
some detainees from being sent to concentration
camps. Having their affidavits only temporarily
delayed his own expulsion from the country.

A leaflet (*Passierschein*) dropped behind German
lines in 1945 by Russian planes two days before
they occupied Modřice, a village outside of
Brno where my mother and I were staying

CHAPTER SIX

Home—Just a Dream

AFTER THE EAR-PIERCING rocket fire the previous night that had almost shook the house from its foundation and my mother's disclosures at dawn, Mother and I lay on our mattress, occupied with our thoughts, trying to get some rest.

I knew my life would never be the same after Mother confirmed what I had felt all along: that I had been an unwanted child. Was that the reason I had not been able to enjoy the same things Lilli did? I knew my parents did not like my association with Herta and Eva and frowned whenever I showed them a piece of our creativity. Was their disapproval part of their reluctance to deal with my existence? I buried that thought almost immediately; I had to tend to the present.

My concern was for Mother. It must have taken great courage or utter despair for her to say these things to me. Although the truth hurt terribly, I knew she had spoken out of concern for me and that she was grateful that I was with her. There were only the two of us and our survival depended on our concern for each other. I had to grow up. I broke the silence to ask whether she knew where Father was now. She did not.

"We have to trust in God," I said to her, noticing tears welling up in her eyes. I put my arms around her. I knew from then on I had to be strong for both of us.

Lying still in the quietness of the early morning hours, we heard horses in the distance. We rushed upstairs to the living room window to get a better look. Then we saw them. Ahead of a colony of black horses and uniformed riders rode an officer on a beautiful white horse. *"So that is what the Russians look like,"* I thought. I had never anticipated their arrival in this way. They came rapidly up the country road, about fifty of them, dressed in traditional Russian military uniforms sitting atop their well-groomed horses. They must have been part of an elite, advanced cavalry group. Several hours later, we saw tanks, trucks, and wagons full of Russian infantry soldiers enter the village, stopping first in the market square and later settling at the farmers' barns and schools. Some pulled into the fields across the road and set up tents, supply wagons, and field kitchens. They were settling in to stay.

Mrs. Peterka, Anna, Mother, and I made ourselves comfortable the best we could in the bunker below. Although Mrs. Peterka had concerns about her husband being upstairs all by himself, we agreed to stay in the bunker until he told us it was all right to leave. Soon we heard the muffled sound of boots above us come and go. We were frightened and anxious to learn what was going on. In the afternoon Mr. Peterka thought we could leave the bunker for a short time while he kept watch at the window. He told us that the Russians, with weapons drawn, were going house to house looking for German soldiers. Civilians were not under their jurisdiction at the present. Because Mr. Peterka spoke some Russian, communication with the soldiers was not difficult, but they questioned everything he said with suspicion and searched every corner of the house including the attic and the basement. Thank God they had not detected the chute to the bunker.

The following evening the soldiers once again went from house to house, this time to "get acquainted." To keep them from questioning Mr. Peterka about his wife's whereabouts, Mrs. Peterka stayed upstairs, helping her husband entertain the troops. Anna, Mother, and I spent that night and many other nights in the bunker.

For the Czechs, these soldiers were liberators and were treated as such. They were welcomed into homes, where the hosts and their guests drank, sang, and danced in celebration of Germany's defeat. They came nightly, in groups of four or five, shouting and waving their canteens as they passed each other on the road. Some were staggering and holding on to each other, somehow making their way from house to house. It was a dangerous situation; their hand-guns and other weapons were never too far from their sight. After partying, they stalked the town, looking for women—capturing and raping young and old alike. We heard of abductions from the village even in broad daylight. No woman was safe, and Mr. Peterka wondered how long he could keep us hidden. In the meantime, we did not go out of the house.

One week after the Russians' arrival, the carousing slowed down enough for us feel safe sleeping in our beds, not the bunker, at night. Ever cautious, however, we still didn't show our faces too freely on the street during the day.

Although the end of the war had not yet been declared, Czech authorities started to reassert their authority by going on a house-to-house survey counting occupants and checking identification papers of all civilians on every property. Mr. Peterka thought they were looking for Germans. Mother reluctantly talked about leaving, saying we had better make our way back to the city; she felt we were putting the Peterka family in danger. Though their behavior towards us did not show it, she thought they no longer saw us as friends—just Germans. I did not share Mother's feelings but could see the emotional and physical toll that the past week had taken on her and complied with her wishes. Early the following morning we packed our small handcart and said goodbye. Our hosts suggested that we stay another week but Mother insisted that we return home. She thought that their hospitality had been more than generous and although we faced an uncertain future, she hoped that someday we would be able to repay them for their kindness. With tears in our eyes, the Peterkas wished us a safe journey and the best for the future. Suppressing her tears, Mrs. Peterka added, "May God go with you."

We knew that as we came closer to the city, acquaintances might recognize us and report to the police that they had seen Germans. Familiar with the countryside in the area, Mother chose to travel through the least inhabited areas—along quiet country roads and fields and through the woods. What were once acres of rich and beautifully planted farms were now barren fields littered with broken-down tanks and burned out trucks. We passed corpses of German soldiers lying next to their dead horses. The field's nauseating odor did not keep Mother from stopping to pray.

It took us most of the day to get into the city. When we came to our house, we found the street completely deserted. About a block away we spotted a couple of Russian soldiers. They saw us and headed our way. Mother quickly pushed the handcart into the backyard and then pulled me with her up the stairs and into our apartment. I crawled into a large empty barrel in the pantry; its door was partially hidden by the bathroom door in front of it. The soldiers quickly made their way up the stairs and asked Mother about my whereabouts; she pretended not to understand. As they searched the apartment, I prayed silently in my hiding place for God to let this danger pass. Unsuccessful in their search, they left the building.

I wondered whether this was our new way of life. Were all Germans free bounty to be hunted down in the victor's view? What had we done to deserve this? We knew it was too dangerous to stay but did not know where to find safe refuge. No one lived in our once vibrant neighborhood. The apartments were empty, ransacked. The doors and windows were open. Window curtains blew freely in the wind. This was no place to live.

Though my parents had taken every precaution in anticipation of the war, neither one of them had thought about what to do once the war was over. As we sat in our cold, empty apartment, Mother said, "We have to see where we can go now, who we could stay with, and where we would be safe." Mother thought that we should wait until dark and then continue to Aunt Mina's apartment, where we might be able to stay. She decided that at nightfall, we could take our handcart and head across town to Aunt Mina's. When we arrived at her apartment building, she was not there and it appeared that she been absent for some time. The floor mat in front of the apartment door was covered with debris and the door knob was dusty. We did find Mrs. Novaková, the Czech apartment house manager, in her downstairs apartment. She had recently returned from the country herself and didn't know of Aunt Mina's whereabouts.

Mrs. Novaková told us that she had joined one of the newly formed Czech government movements whose primary function was to bring order into the city. Even so, she assured us that because she was sympathetic to our situation and had known us for so many years, we could trust her. Mother wasn't sure, but had no other choice, so she asked Mrs. Novaková where we could stay. She answered, "Look in the back yard." There we found an old garden shed. We noticed the peeling plaster on the outside, but the single window—still covered with blackout shades—was intact and the roof appeared to be in good condition. The room was about twelve by twelve feet. As I opened the dusty window and looked over a small garden, the refreshing scent of lilac came in and filled the shed, reminding me of the garden at home. The inside walls were exposed brick, without plaster. On the floor we found an old, dirty mattress. "We can clean this place up," Mother said. "We need only a few things—a small stove, some new hinges and a lock for the door." With Mrs. Novaková's help we cleaned up the shed and settled in late that night.

Within twenty-four hours of changing residence, people were required to report their new address to the authorities. When Mother and I reported ours the following morning, we were first given white armbands, identifying us as Germans. Then we were told that all of our civil rights had been revoked. At first, Mother looked at the official with a bewildered look, not understanding what she had just heard. There must be a mistake. After all, we were all born in this country and all of our ancestors lived within a few miles of this city. How could it be that we not only had lost all of our possessions but were disowned by our home country as well? The official looked at Mother, his eyes reflecting hate and anger and said, "Now you can clean up the destruction you and your fellow Germans created." Then he described our daily duties as ordered by the new government: to clean up the aftermath of this terrible war—unpaid work reserved for Germans.

My new workplace, the Russian Military Headquarters, was within walking distance of our shed. Every morning, I reported to a Russian lady officer who gave me my assignment for the day. One morning it would be to clean up debris from a few rooms on the ground floor, destroyed by bombs. Other days I carried bricks and pieces of mortar to the outside of the building for pick up.

My supervisor did not speak Czech and I did not speak Russian. We communicated using gestures and in the process became fond of each other. Whenever I came in the morning, she would smile, calling me by my name and I would return the greeting in Czech with "Dobrý den," (good day). One day, around noon, she took me to the bathroom, locked the door, and left. Not knowing what to expect, I was frightened. After a while she came with a large plate of food and motioned for me to eat. I had not seen so much wonderful food since my birthday at the Peterka's house. Later that day, just before I finished my work, she handed me a package of food and motioned for me to hide it in my clothing. When I returned to the shed that evening with the bundle of food, Mother was so surprised; she had not had a meal in days.

The next day, once again the officer brought lunch to the bathroom. She could not give me food openly and only after the office closed could I go home undetected. Before weekends and holidays, she gave me enough food for several days. We did not go hungry. One evening, just before I was ready to go home, she tapped my feet with a stick and pointed at my worn down shoes. The laces were torn and one of the soles had a big hole. She turned to her desk and picked up a pair of sturdy army boots and heavy socks and gave them to me. "I hope they fit," she gestured. I smiled, placing my hand on my chest saying, "Děkuji," (thank you). And then I remembered what Mother had said months ago when we emptied our pantry feeding our homeless relatives: "If you share during others' time of need, God will provide in yours." Our blessings came to us in small doses; nevertheless, we were grateful for each one.

On May 8, 1945, Germany officially surrendered. It was instantaneously declared a national holiday. Russian military trucks filled the streets while exhilarated Russian soldiers and Czech partisan groups drank to their country's success. Soldiers shot their rifles and machine guns skyward while the crowds cheered and shouted. Smoke from the gunfire filled the air; streamers cascaded from the buildings. Russian soldiers as well as Czechs, young and old, danced in the streets to Russian folk music.

On the other side of the city, a mob of young Czechs marched to one of the local radio stations shouting, "Smrt Němcum," (death to Germans) and "Němci Ven," (Germans out).

Mrs. Novaková came and suggested that we stay inside our shed for a few days—"till the streets get back to normal." She brought us a newspaper so we could see the headlines for ourselves. That day the front page of *Narodni Politica*, a Prague newspaper, showed a picture of Hitler covering the whole front page with the caption in Czech: "The Führer has Fallen." The main article on the following page gave an account of the retaliation German capitulation forces experienced. They were under orders to leave the city. Prague had been declared an exit city for all retreating forces, safeguarded by the International Red Cross. As they attempted to leave, however, Czech revolutionary guard members surrounded and captured the first group of soldiers, not under protection yet, tied them to light poles along Main Street, doused them with gasoline and ignited their bodies. German civilians, who were also under the protection of the Red Cross and wanted to leave, were captured, beaten, robbed—and then murdered. Other retreating German forces attempting to cross the Elbe River were cut off on the bridge, shot, and thrown into the river below.

My stomach heaved when I read of these horrible atrocities and I wondered, *"Oh God, when will this hatred end?"* I had waited for the end of the war for six years, never dreaming it would end this way. Peace was certainly not in sight. Not for us, anyway.

CHAPTER SEVEN

Brno Death March

DR. EDVARD BENEŠ, the president of Czechoslovakia, had planned events that followed Germany's surrender many years before. After the September 1938 Munich Agreement, he resigned from his presidency and moved to England. In London he established a government in exile, the first step of which would be, upon readmission to his homeland, to declare the Munich Pact invalid so that the borders drawn in 1919 by the Treaty of Saint Germain could be reestablished.

He stated that in order to restore Czechoslovakia to its original borders, all Germans would have to be expelled ("transferred" was the diplomatic word) in order to prevent a resurfacing of the country's ethnic problems. By 1942, the British and in 1943, the American and Russian governments agreed, and plans to that end were soon taking shape. What was to become the largest movement of people in European history had begun before the final plans were defined. Although the Allies agreed that these "transfers" be made in a most humane and civilized way, they were not.

It seemed that our destiny was sealed before that fateful day of May 30, 1945, the Catholic holiday of Corpus Christi. At that time there were still twenty-five to thirty thousand Germans living in Brno. From the estimated sixty-thousand German inhabitants in our city during the war, about half had left before the last conflict.

On the evening before Corpus Christi, members of the young revolutionary Czech guard, a newly formed partisan group, and other self-appointed groups marched through the city streets with bullhorns in hand, calling for all German citizens to gather outside their homes by 8:00 p.m. and to bring one piece of hand luggage. We were told that the Czech president was coming to the city for three days and for security reasons the government wanted all German citizens out of the city during his visit. Though we wondered why we were suddenly summoned this way, everyone complied. We did not question orders of the new Communist regime, just as we had not questioned the last dictatorship. This was not a democracy.

Once outside our homes, we were ordered to line up in rows of eight. When Mother and I looked around to make sense of what was happening, we saw Mrs. Novaková, our apartment house manager, looking out of her window and with a waving motion to me as if to say, "Don't worry." Mother looked at her, shrugging her shoulders, indicating that she did not understand the reason for this gathering, but was not worried. In front of me, a woman was struggling to carry her suitcase and her two babies. I offered to help; though grateful, she declined. Next to Mother were two elderly women, one of them in a wheelchair. I knew it would not be easy, wherever we were going, for her to travel in her chair.

The crowd, ordered to walk quickly and follow the guards, was flanked by uniformed men whose faces reflected hatred and anger. By nightfall we came to a police training station and its small stadium in one of the suburbs of town. Yelling, "Jdeme, jdeme" (move, move), the guards pushed us through the narrow gate into the small administration building. Filed in a single line, we passed a desk with two guards holding large metal boxes in which we had to place everything we had of value: money, jewelry, and whatever else the guards wanted. We were then shoved through a narrow hallway onto the training field. One guard, using his bullhorn, shouted with a sarcastic voice, "Have a good night." Two others, overcome with sinister laughter, slammed the gates shut and fastened the locks. Then the reflector lights high above the stands went out; we were to spend the night outside in darkness.

We spread out the small blanket Mother had brought, but the damp grass soon penetrated our clothing. We did not rest that chilly night in May and neither did the armed guards in the stands watching us. It was too dark to see who lay around us, but we could hear babies crying and I imagined our frail, elderly neighbors shivering through the night. At the first hint of morning light, we were ordered to gather our things and move out.

"Jdeme, jdeme, richle, richle," (move, move, hurry, hurry) the guards shouted, prodding the slowest with their rifle butts. No one was allowed to stop, talk, or slow down. Still in rows of eight or ten, we were marched passed the city limits with two guards on either side. Other groups from different parts of the city joined ours until the human train grew into thousands.

As we moved along the highway, church bells chimed throughout the city in observance of Corpus Christi. I thought of this day in years past, when, in my prettiest church dress, I had joined other Catholics in the customary procession. This year we were dressed in wet, dirty clothes; it must have been the longest, saddest holiday procession God had ever seen in our city. I prayed for Him to go with us and protect us.

Once we were on the open highway, too far from any facility that could accommodate thousands of people, the thought occurred to me that we were not just going out of town because of the President's visit. We were being herded like wild animals. Where were we going and why?

These questions went through my mind as the long procession moved along the highway in the heat of the noonday sun. It was an unseasonably hot day and our food and water rations were nearly gone. Even so, we kept moving; we had no choice. Shouting profanities, the guards pushed the elderly, weary from hours of walking, to the side of the road. One elderly woman sitting on her suitcase by the side of the road was mercilessly clubbed for no reason. Outraged by the Nazis' atrocities, the Czechs were lashing out at innocent, defenseless people. There was nothing that could justify such treatment. Nothing.

I had so many questions but no answers. All I knew was that we were in danger and could not protect ourselves. A short distance away, I saw women with crying babies who were wet, thirsty, hot, and hungry. No one was allowed to speak or help these mothers. We had to keep moving.

Along the road stood onlookers who spat at us and screamed, "Němci ven" (Germans out). I was afraid to look at them and tried not to let these expressions touch my heart.

Once we were several miles outside the city and on the open two-lane highway, some people, too exhausted to continue, collapsed on the side of the road. The guards insisted on keeping the lines at least six abreast and having people move up to fill the gaps. Some children who were separated from their mothers screamed, desperate to be protected. It was utter chaos. The less control the guards had over the crowds, the more aggressive and angry they became. Their endless curses convinced them that they had the upper hand. "Deutsche Schweine," (German pigs) one shouted at us.

Mother and I were toward the end of the long procession. I could see many people lying in the shade of the chestnut trees that lined the highway—exhausted and crying for water. Some were too sick to continue; for others, the shade had come too late. We could not count our countrymen and women; some lay dead in the ditches, their clothing stained with blood from a senseless beating. Their belongings were thrown all over the highway, and those of us who could still walk were not allowed to stop and mourn their loss. We had to keep moving. Local Czechs were plundering through the bags and suitcases that lay in the ditches, belongings of the dead who lay beside their meager possessions.

As night fell, the elderly that remained had difficulty navigating the bumpy road. In years past, some of them had been successful and energetic businesspeople whose hard work had helped build our vibrant city. Today, in the eyes of the guards, they were worthless and nameless. Mother, unable to bear seeing all the indignity and pain around her, started to cry. Afraid her compassion would attract the guard's attention, I whispered to her to please be quiet. We managed to go unnoticed.

As we trudged along, we noticed a guard driving down the road on a motorcycle calling out "Jdeme" (move) to a man who was walking alone in the middle of the roadway. When the man did not respond, the guard shot him in the back and drove past. As we came closer, we saw that the dead man was carrying a sign on his chest that read "taub" (deaf). Later that evening a passing thunderstorm brought welcomed relief from the heat. Parched and weak, I held out my hands to catch some of the water to drink. The army boots the Russian officer had given me, now filled with water, felt very heavy, but I was afraid to stop and empty them. Mother was close to exhaustion; her face was very pale and perspiration stood on her forehead. I wondered where we were going and how many more steps we could take. All I knew was that we were on the main highway between Brno and Vienna and that somehow I needed to be strong enough for both of us.

Every hour or so, an open panel truck passed by to collect bodies from both sides of the road. On one of these stops, two guards lifted an old man onto the truck. I could not tell whether he was alive or dead. One of the guards stopped for a moment, lifted his handgun to the man's head, and pulled the trigger. "Ten už nemůže," (He can't anymore), the guard said to the other. Mother reached for my hand and I squeezed hers. What were we witnessing?

In the middle of the night the long human train came to a stop. We had reached the outskirts of Pohořelice, a village close to the Austrian border, approximately thirty-five kilometers from Brno. By the side of the road was a concrete mile marker that I asked Mother to sit on to get some rest.

Why had we stopped? People around us started whispering and rumors spread quickly that the Czechs had planned to hand us over to the Austrians, who were turning us away. And now our captors were refusing to take us back. Some women started crying; others looked too exhausted to care. Close by, a man argued in open defiance with one of the guards who swung his rifle off his shoulders and beat the man beyond recognition. Hundreds of us watched, unable to do anything. Mother and I closed our eyes and plugged our ears, trying to erase what we had witnessed. Mother looked ash white. To keep her from fainting, I wiped her face with a wet piece of clothing. "Hold on to me," I told her, completely disregarding the orders not to speak. Desperately tired, we leaned on each other for fearing of falling to the ground.

Soon we heard guards approaching. They separated the crowd into two groups. Those who were unable to continue, Mother and I among them, were directed into the desolate fields a short distance off the road towards five huge storage buildings that had once belonged to an agricultural experimental station. We later learned that the other group stayed on the road and continued walking towards Austria, where they found safety and ultimately settled.

Our group of several thousand weary people made its way across the fifty-plus acres of farmland into the abandoned buildings. Their tall, high rolling steel doors stood open. Some had silos attached that had received bombing damage; two of the buildings had blown off roofs and three had no windows. What these hot, foul-smelling shelters had in common was what they lacked: floors, blankets, food and water. We found a spot in one of the buildings, close to the door, spread our small blanket on the dusty floor, and stretched out. After the thirty-hour march, getting off our feet was the best thing that could have happened to us. We had only one small blanket and the clothes on our backs. Unhurt and alive, I thanked God for the blessing of rest.

The next day the guards designated one of the buildings as an infirmary where they carried sick people on makeshift stretchers. The building was filled to capacity, but there were no medical personnel or priests to attend the sick and dying—just guards.

That night Mother and I, though exhausted, could not sleep; the cries and moaning coming from the helpless patients next door haunted us. Even more disturbing was listening to women screaming as Russian soldiers carried them off to rape them in the open fields. Fearing that the next night the soldiers would come to our building, women wore disguises that made them look old and unattractive. They used dirt to ashen their hair and faces and rolled in the dust to dirty their clothing. That evening, two sixteen year olds and I hid in the silo ducts. The soldiers made their rounds with flashlights to carry off unsuspecting sleeping women. The disguises worked and my hiding place was never detected.

On the third day in camp, my survival instinct set in. "I am going to see if I can find some work and get something to eat," I told Mother. "Just be careful," she warned. Some Romanian soldiers had set up a soup kitchen for our camp, but there was not enough food for the thousands of displaced people there. Mother and I had not eaten anything except watered down soup for more than three days. First I volunteered to help transport or tend to the sick. "You're not strong enough," one guard answered as he lifted a stretcher and walked toward the sick ward. I had heard that a dysentery and typhus epidemic had set into the camp and that there was no medicine available to bring the sick comfort or relief. But it was not until I saw the rows upon rows of dying patients crying out for help that I understood the toll the epidemics were taking: one hundred people died each day. The stench left me nauseated and dizzy. When I asked the guard where the dead were being buried, he pointed towards the main road. Although I looked in that direction, I could not see a cemetery. Confused, I did not ask again.

On my way back to our building I saw some farmhouses outside the experimental station boundaries. As I came closer to one of them, I saw Romanian soldiers cooking in the backyard. I stopped at the fence, mesmerized by the smell of food. One of the soldiers motioned, asking me whether I was hungry. I nodded. He smiled and gave me an army canteen full of food. I did not know what language to use that he would understand, so I just smiled at him, held my hand over my chest and nodded my head. He smiled back at me and nodded his head; he understood. As I left, he motioned for me to come back the next day. I nodded my head. Mother cried for joy when I came back to her with some hot food. The Lord had provided again.

After a week at camp, we had regained some strength. Mother and I were called to the main guard's office and told to collect our things; we were going back home. The officer added in a very sarcastic and hateful tone, "Mrs. Novaková is responsible for your return. She must have powerful connections." She did, I thought, looking heavenward, but not the sort he imagined.

Several hours later, Mother and I climbed on an open panel truck. Just the thought of leaving that place was liberating. As the truck drove through the fields towards the main road, I could feel every bump but did not care. We drove towards home on the same dusty highway we had just traversed. I thought of the people whose deaths I had witnessed, of the children crying in utter terror, and of the exhausted elderly bludgeoned for not keeping the pace.

Today the highway was empty and the sky was clear and blue. As we rode, images of what I had experienced somehow started to fade and a soothing calm came over me, almost as if God had spread a blanket over my fears and whispered, "Be still, I have everything under control." I was grateful to no longer witness the brutal atrocities, the many sick and dying I had never imagined possible and yearned to know how God viewed the inhumanity I had witnessed. I did not receive an answer until many years later.

It didn't take but a couple of hours on the truck to get back to the city. Exhausted, hungry, and dirty, we arrived home. Our garden shed looked like a wonderful palace welcoming us.

CHAPTER EIGHT

Father Is Alive!

THE FOLLOWING MORNING, when Mrs. Nováková realized we were back, she knocked on our door. "Oh, I am so glad to see you," she said, her hand reaching out and touching Mother's face. "I was worried when you didn't return the evening you were gathered outside the house," she continued. "Come upstairs to take a nice hot bath while I fix you breakfast. While we eat, I will fill you in on what happened here while you were gone."

Clean for the first time in weeks, we sat at her kitchen table enjoying some coffee and freshly baked bread with jam. "When I heard that the government was determined to expel all ethnic Germans from the country, I contacted a few political friends on your behalf," she said. "My brother, who had recently received a promotion in the newly formed Communist Party government, also pulled strings to bring you back. He thought that although you are Germans, you should have no problem staying in the country. From the documents and affidavits you showed me, I am certain of it." With tears in her eyes, Mother said,"I wish we could repay you and your brother for all your kindness." Mrs. Nováková reassured her that our debt had been paid by my Father's helping her countrymen.

Though we had finished our meal, we kept talking. Mother explained what had happened since our forced exodus. Mother left out some of the graphic details of the torture and killing we had witnessed. "We saw many exhausted, mostly elderly people by the side of the road, holding on to their bags with one hand and motioning the passing guards with the other, begging them for water." Mrs. Nováková just shook her head in disbelief. "The people should have been told that they were being expelled, and the elderly should have been transported to at least the border." I looked at her and knew she didn't know the half of it, but I did not say anything.

Later Mother told me that she felt best to leave out some of the details of the harrowing experience in order not to hurt Mrs. Novaková's newly acquired national pride. Mother added, "One day, God will be the judge of what happened there and the individuals who were responsible." Before leaving the apartment, Mrs. Novaková gave us much needed provisions such as bread, eggs, potatoes, and fresh green vegetables, as well as cooking oil—all of which we readily accepted; our cabinets were empty.

Our arms full and bodies tired, Mother and I returned to the shed for some rest. Soon we heard a knock on the door. I went to open it.

It was Father!

We held him close, looking at him repeatedly, not believing it was really him. All through the night we listened to what had happened to him since we had last seen him in December 1944—six months earlier. "After my arrest, I didn't think I was ever going to see you again," he told us. "The Germans accused me of collaborating with the enemy by helping the detainees. I didn't know what proof they had but thought they would shoot me immediately." I noticed Mother's eyes welling up at the thought that she could have lost her husband. "By February," Father continued, "most of the German officials had either been recalled to Germany or had left the Protectorate in a hurry to escape the advancing Russians. The political structure of the German Reich was disintegrating. When the day of German capitulation came, I learned that my arresting papers had not yet been processed; they had been casually thrown into an official's desk drawer at Gestapo headquarters in Brno, where I had been held since my arrest. I could not believe the bureaucratic oversight. Or was it divine intervention?" I looked at Mother, who just nodded her head.

"After German operations had ceased at headquarters," Father continued, "only a few guards and prisoners were left to fend for themselves. Orders regarding the prisoners may have been given, but at this point, the guards, now without authority and anxious about their own safety, ignored the commands. "I will always re-member," Father continued, "that amidst all the cruelty, there was a thread of kindness woven into my days. Good and evil-side by side."

He went on to tell us about a guard who had made his life tolerable by keeping him updated on outside events and bringing him extra food. This same guard released him from his cell with a clean set of clothing and wished him luck in his search for us. The man, a local German resident himself, feared for his own safety, now that the regime had changed hands. He told Father of his plans to make it, any way he could, to the Austrian border. Because he spoke only a little Czech, he had to avoid human contact as much as possible. His hope was that freight trains headed towards the border would be in operation and that he could jump aboard and go unnoticed, the sixty kilometers to the border. Father wished him well; he never found out whether the soldier made it. This man's precarious journey mirrored Europe's instability. Who belonged where?

Knowing that the Czech officials were looking out for all Germans to clear their country of their century-old enemy, Father carefully mapped out his search for us. It took him several weeks to find us. First he looked for us in Modřice. We were not there. Mr. Peterka told him that we had gone back home. He encircled the city, just as Mother and I had, to keep from being recognized as German or raise suspicion. When he reached our apartment building, he found it empty and no one who could give him information as to our whereabouts. He waited for nightfall and then headed out into the country again, hoping that his brother-in-law Theodore would know where we were. Father was certain to find him home. When Mother asked how her brother and family were, Father explained that Theodore had slammed the door in his face and refused his request for water.

Before the war, my Father's Austrian roots had been irrelevant; now, they filled Uncle Theodore with anger and fear. Father was no longer a beloved relative but a political enemy. All Father could do was speak to him through a crack in the door. Angry and dejected, Father spent daylight hours resting in nearby woods and mapping out the next place to search; nights he spent foraging for food. He lived the life of a fugitive.

After a few days' rest in the fields and nearby forest, he made his way back to the city, continuing his search. Most apartment buildings were still empty; former occupants had either fled the country before the last battle or still lived in the country with other relatives. Then he came to Aunt Mina's apartment house. As he approached the building, Mrs. Nováková recognized him and showed him where we were. And now we sat in our small shed exchanging experiences. Father turned to me and said, "Margit, during the time I was working for the Germans I was not allowed to tell anyone the truth about the work I was involved in. I was sworn to secrecy and did not realize the scope of treachery, lies, and brutality the Nazis were capable of. But I can live the rest of my life with a clear conscience that I have not taken a human life or mistreated anyone."

He continued, telling us how he started helping prisoners by bringing them news from home. Once he was certain that none of the officers spoke or understood Czech, he then helped the detainees during interrogations by changing some of their answers if he felt they were too incriminating. Somehow the Germans discovered his stealth. In the fall of 1944, the Gestapo colonel in charge began getting suspicious and started investigating him. By the end, Father had helped at least thirty people. In some cases he had prolonged their time in custody, thereby preventing their transport to concentration camps.

We told Father about being herded to the Austrian border and the various ways Germans were being attacked. "I pray, with God's help, we may get through this," Mother added. It was almost morning when we finally settled in for a long, sound sleep. I spread a blanket and pillow on the floor close to the door, leaving the mattress to my parents. It was a little crowded in the shed that night, but we made do. We were happy to be together as a family.

The following morning, once again, we had to register our change of residency. Mrs. Nováková suggested that we take along some proof that we were not "enemies of the state." Mother thought that the affidavits and letters from families of detainees Father had helped during the war would provide the necessary evidence. When we arrived at the registrar's office and Father gave the officer our identification, he looked at the documents and went to another room, where another official waved for us to come in.

I could tell from the appearance of the room that the officer there had a more official position than the registrar in the front lobby. The oversized desk almost filled the room. There were two chairs facing it, but the officer did not ask my parents to sit down. He was a short, bald-headed, middle-aged man with glasses and an authoritative, stern look. As he sat down in his leather chair, he looked at the documents Father had given to him, briefly examined the affidavits, and said, "Until we can verify the authenticity of these affidavits, we will have to keep you and your wife in our custody." Father told him that he had been in Gestapo custody until the end of the war because of the activities mentioned in the letters. "That will have to be verified. You don't have any release papers," the official responded. He turned around and with a wave of his hand two guards came in to handcuff my parents and take them away. We were shocked. Not even in our worst imagination had we thought this might happen. Before Mother followed the guards out the door, she handed me her pouch, her hands shaking and her face ashen with fear. I was not allowed to say goodbye to her or to my father. Then the officer turned to me and said, "You can go home."

Fear and anger gripped my heart. As my eyes followed my parents, flanked by guards who didn't even know their names, the tears came. I was on my own. As I walked home, I had flashbacks of the last month—the epidemic outbreak of dysentery and typhus and the ashen-white faces of the dead people all around me along the roadside and later in camp. I needed an outlet for my towering rage about all the pain that I had witnessed and now the injustice of losing my parents. Was this hatred I felt for the Czechs the same as what they felt towards me, an ethnic German? Overwhelmed by this toxic loathing, I turned to hating myself, my life, the day I was born, and even God.

How could He allow so much pain and suffering to exist? I had no answers and could not bring myself to pray.

As I turned the corner of our street, my thoughts and feelings were interrupted by voices singing an old hymn, *"Oh God, Our Help in Ages Past."* I hadn't heard church music in over a year. The music was coming from a hall in one of the buildings that served as a meeting place for the Salvation Army. I stopped and heard them singing, *"Our Shelter from the Stormy Blast."* The music brought back memories of our organist playing that hymn in our church after it was bombed. The whole front entrance, including the steeple of the Gothic structure, had been destroyed, but the organ, located above one of the side altars, was saved. The organist, expressing his gratitude, played that hymn the day after the bombing.

Since the door to the meetinghouse was open, I walked in slowly, not knowing whether I, a German wearing a white armband, would be welcomed.

A woman by the door motioned for me to come in and sit down. She smiled and nodded when she saw my white band.

I was safe.

The speaker, a tall, dark-haired man, about sixty, took the stand and looked out at his audience of about fifty. Someone handed me a set of scriptures, open to Psalm 27, which the speaker was reading.

The Lord is my light and my salvation; whom shall I fear? The Lord is the strength of my life; of whom shall I be afraid?

It seemed as if the speaker spoke only to me, his eyes meeting mine.

For in the time of trouble he shall hide me in his pavilion... And now shall mine head be lifted up above mine enemies round about me...

I felt the tears rolling down my face; I could no longer control my emotions. What had I done? I had let anger towards God enter my heart. It was He who had sent Uncle Hugo and my friends Herta and Eva into my life to help me grow. It was He who had provided for and protected me all these years. In that humble, small meeting room I broke down and asked God for forgiveness, promising never to question Him again.

The presiding Salvation Army officer spoke with me after the meeting. With a gentle, soothing voice he asked me to come to his apartment and meet his wife. I accepted his invitation. Major Emma Korbel was a soft-spoken lady with bright, twinkling eyes, slightly graying hair, and a beautiful smile. She told me that she too was German and that her husband was British. They had just recently been allowed into the country and assigned to our city. After I told them my story and the circumstances of my entering their meetinghouse, Major Korbel asked me to return any time I felt the need.

Before I left that evening, she gave me a copy of The New Testament and Psalms, in German. I had never owned a book of scriptures before. I felt strengthened and assured that the Lord had forgiven me for my lack of faith that afternoon. To this day, that book brings back memories of a couple God had placed in my life when I needed courage the most.

With new faith and resolve, I settled into my daily routine. My new work assignment was across town. Every morning I walked three miles to the residence of a young prominent Czech couple, the Kubčics. My job was to babysit their four-year-old boy and his six-month-old sister. I enjoyed this assignment and had no difficulty keeping this active boy entertained in the back yard of their beautiful home. Every day at noon, Mr. Kubčic came home for lunch. The first thing he did was turn on his radio to listen to Glenn Miller's daily BBC program. I enjoyed the swinging rhythm of this new music and wondered what the country was like that produced such upbeat and carefree music.

Mrs. Kubčicová was a young, slender woman. Her long, beautiful black hair was always braided and tied in a bun. She frequently hosted dinners for her husband's business clients. I remember seeing her on one occasion dressed in a long sleeve, lavender silk dress with a deep neckline and a beautiful string of pearl necklace that nearly reached her waist. She looked stunning. Mrs. Kubčicová was about my height, and during the time I worked for her and her husband she gave me clothes that she no longer wanted. Although some of the outfits were too elegant for my simple life, I was able to wear two of them for special occasions at church meetings.

Soon after I started working for the Kubčics, I learned of my parents' location. Mrs. Novaková explained that I could not see my mother but was allowed to write and send certain items such as toiletries, clothing, and food. I was not allowed any contact with my father; he was considered a political prisoner. The first thing

I sent to Mother was a handwritten copy of Psalm 27 and a hand-made birthday card. I remembered how the Psalm had changed my outlook and had given me comfort and strength. I imagined that Mother and her fellow inmates could use the same. In her letter that followed she told me that my gift had consoled everyone there and that some of the women cried as they listened to my letters every week. They considered me an angel bringing light into their darkness. My correspondence with Mother and her new friends brought relief to us all. I wished I could have felt the same connection to my father.

Winter came earlier than expected that year. During the first part of October, I saw the first snowflakes fall and worried about how to keep warm during the upcoming winter months. Mrs. Nováková had already anticipated my need. One day she brought a small pot-belly stove to the shed and had her son install it. She then supplied me with some coal and kindling supplies, some of which were hard to come by as everything was rationed. Mrs. Nováková said that she had connections and would be able to bring me a small amount every week. I was so grateful. If I were conservative, I would be all right during the cold winter months ahead.

I did not want to think of Christmas that year. This first holiday celebration after the war was somber in many homes; almost every family had experienced the loss of someone dear or had lost their homes and possessions. I felt bereft. Mrs. Nováková and her son were visiting with her brother and the Kubčic family was traveling to see relatives in the country.

I walked home from my job the afternoon of Christmas Eve knowing that no one would be waiting for me at the garden shed. I picked up a twig of greenery from the sidewalk and as I passed an overflowing garbage container on one of the street corners, a small piece of candle fell out in front of my feet. I casually kicked it to the side and then decided to pick it up and take it home.

As I approached my shelter for the night, I could see that the window was covered with icy crystals. I opened the door; the room was as cold as the frosty flowers on the glass pane. The beautiful designs reminded me of the hours I spent as a child playing with the icy windows, until my fingers were capped with frost. However, soon the frost would melt away—along with my childhood fantasies. I could not decide whether to use up my ration of wood and coal that night or wait until the next day. I opted to wait. After all, tomorrow was Christmas Day.

Before going to bed, I put the green twig in a bottle, placed the stubble of a candle in front of it, and lit the candle. A faint glow threw soft shadows into the small, cold room as I lay there trying to get warm. The joy of Christmas seemed so far away. There were no presents under a tree tonight and I could not smell any good food or hear any music or laughter. Suddenly, I thought I heard someone read the Christmas story. The voice sounded like Uncle Hugo's. As the candle slowly burned down and the shadows dimmed, I fell asleep—content and safe.

God has not let me forget that lonely Christmas night. For whenever I am discontent or unsatisfied, He brings it to my mind—Christmas Eve of 1945.

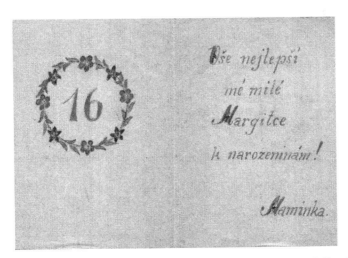

My first book of scriptures, the Psalms and New Testament in German, was given to me in 1945 when I needed their guidance and comfort the most.

A handmade birthday card my mother sent to me while she was in captivity and I was living alone in Mrs. Novaková's shed. I received the card on my sixteenth birthday.

CHAPTER NINE

From a Shed to a Camp

NEWLY FORMED ICICLES on the windowpanes greeted me as I looked out from under the blankets the next morning. The small tree in the garden, decorated with new icicles and capped with fresh snow, reminded me of a Christmas tree. It was beautiful to watch as the sun touched the branches and transformed the snow particles into colored crystal ornaments.

I was glad I had saved my ration of wood and coal for this day. For now, I stayed in bed to keep warm, watch the tree, and think of my family and Christmases past. At times I found myself laughing while remembering funny stories Father shared with us on those cold holiday nights.

Later that day it started snowing again and I thought of little Petr Kubčic, who could hardly wait until he came back to the city after the holidays. I had promised to play snowball games with him when he returned. Before Christmas, we had enjoyed our time together rolling down the embankment of the hilly property, laughing, and chasing each other. I knew I would miss this playtime with him whenever my employment there would come to an end; he had become a pleasant distraction from my worries and concerns. Survival on my own and the responsibility of being the only "link to the outside" for my parents lay heavily on my mind.

In mid-February, I received a summons to appear for questioning before the Czech government authorities. Mrs. Novaková suggested I bring the few remaining letters and other documents that we had not brought with us when my parents appeared before them the first time. She also suggested I take some pictures of the family. I did not understand why, but she had been right the last time she had offered advice about which items to bring, so I did as she suggested.

Almost a whole year had passed since I sat in the same waiting room. When my turn came, I stood before the same bald-headed officer. Once again, I could barely suppress my anger toward this powerful man. Even so, I felt prepared. Not quite sixteen years of age, I felt like David facing Goliath. I was ready for battle.

First he talked about my brother Erwin, alleging he had been a member of Hitler's elite SS squad. I looked at him wondering where he came up with his stories and asked him, "Why are you saying these things to me, knowing they aren't true? You know that he was in the infantry. I have a photograph to prove it." I reached into my handbag and handed him a photograph of Erwin in his military uniform. "You know very well," I continued, "that as a German, he was drafted into the military and did not hide in the Underground like some." The officer looked at me but did not respond. I could not read his expressionless face. He then asked me the same questions he had asked Father about his activity. Instead of answering, I asked him whether or not he had checked out Father's whereabouts since 1944.

I again reached into my bag. This time I handed him the remainder of the letters my parents had left. "Is that proof enough of his activity?" I asked the officer, "And don't tell me you have to verify these. All of them have original signatures." I handed him three affidavits from families of individuals whom my Father had helped. I surprised myself at my courage talking in this manner to an official in the Czech government. Again, he did not say a word and showed no emotion. He was well trained in interrogations. After a long pause, he looked at me and asked, "Would you like to continue your education?"

"Of course I would," I answered promptly, not knowing why he had asked that question.

"My government has an offer to make to you," he continued. "We are going to educate you, free of charge, and give you free room and board." I looked at him, waiting for the rest of the offer. *There has to be a catch*, I thought. He did not say anything. "What about my parents?" I asked. "Where will they be?" "We are going to send them to West Germany," he answered. My response came quickly as I shook my head, "Oh no," I said. "You can keep your education and everything else, thank you very much. I can get an education elsewhere. Where my parents go, I will go also. You have separated enough families. You're not going to separate mine."

His eyes showed anger and his hands started trembling. Surprisingly, he did not call the guards or arrest me for being so outspoken. I could not believe my audacity and did not dare imagine the consequences my outburst could have. Unnerved by my defiance, he abruptly said, "We will notify you of the government's decision." He then stood up and left the room. I was left alone to consider what kind of decision the government was going to make. If they wanted to deport my parents to West Germany, why would they want to keep me here?

In my letter to Mother I could tell her only so much without having the letter confiscated or its contents heavily censured. From her reply I had the feeling that she understood what had happened.

I went about my daily routine, waiting for an answer from the government. Days turned to weeks. February turned into March and April. No answer.

Springtime came early in 1946. Each morning I opened the shed's window, which faced Mrs. Nováková's flower garden, to enjoy the fresh air. The small tree outside my window started budding, and the first bees buzzed around looking for nectar. Beautiful yellow and white daffodils filled two flowerbeds under the window. I wished I could send a bouquet to Mother. It would have reminded her of home.

For my birthday in April I received a card from her, made of yellow, plain stock paper and colored with crayons. I was surprised that she could draw so beautifully. Growing up I had never noticed this talent.

On the same day, an official letter from the government arrived, ordering me to report on May 1, 1946, with baggage no heavier than 50 kilogram to the former German detention camp in Maloměřice for transport to the Federal Republic of Germany. Anxious about what would become of my parents, I ran to Mrs. Novaková and asked whether she could find out if my parents were going with me. She promised to try.

The next two weeks passed slowly. I waited for her knock on the door to give me the news I was so eager to hear, but there was no knock. Finally, two days before I was to leave, she came to tell me she was unable to find out anything. I was shocked and devastated, with a thousand questions going through my mind. How could I pack everything not knowing if my parents, forced to stay behind, might upon release need their few remaining belongings? On the other hand, what if they were also taken to the camp and I met them empty-handed?

I did not know what to do. I did not want to go alone into a strange country, knowing my parents were locked up here indefinitely, for no reason. There were so many unanswered, difficult questions. And even if I knew which items to take, how would I transport them? I went to bed but only tossed and turned. Then I remembered Uncle Hugo and one of his favorite sayings, a piece of scripture, which he always hummed like a melody: *"Cast thy burden upon the Lord . . ."* Before I was able to finish reciting the verse, I fell asleep.

The following morning, I felt that I had received all the answers and everything was clear in my mind. Had I dreamed? I don't know. I remembered that our small handcart was still behind the shed and in perfect condition. I asked Mrs. Novaková for some heavy thread with which I sewed up one of the blankets to make a huge sack. I placed it on the cart; it fit perfectly. I was ready to pack.

Confident that everything would be all right, I placed all the things we had accumulated that year into the handmade sack: warm items that we would need the following winter—among them my army boots and a pair of heavy shoes for Mother; a couple of pots and cups, plates and eating utensils for three; and three blankets and pillows. Mrs. Novaková gave me a few towels from her closet and three bars of soap. I was grateful to her for the soap as it was rationed. Then I packed Mother's pouch with mementos that had survived the war—letters, pictures and, of course, Uncle Hugo's diary. When I finished, the sack was full and the cart was heavy.

The next morning, the day I was to report to the camp, I went and said goodbye to Mrs. Novaková, the woman without whom I could not have survived. It was difficult for me to find the right words to say to her. As tears came to my eyes, she smiled, put her index finger to my lips, and shook her head. "Don't say anything," she said. "Just remember me in your prayers." I promised I would. As I made my round of goodbyes, I stopped by Major Korbel and my friends at the Salvation Army. There were seven of us in the small chapel, offering a prayer for my journey and the days ahead for all of us.

As I pushed my cart through the city streets, I tried to put to memory all that I saw around me. St. Peter's Cathedral looked down on me as if to say, "Farewell, dear friend. You'll be all right." Slowly, as I put distance between the old familiar places and my unknown destination, I realized that I was not going to see the city ever again. My documents read, "Permanently expelled from Czechoslovakia." Many memories were not pleasant ones, but this was home— the place where I had grown up, the city I loved. My own government had decided to disown and expel all ethnic Germans—people who had contributed to the economy, education, and culture of this area for hundreds of years.

I started walking a little faster, hoping to erase the bitterness that started to choke me. I began humming a melody and then another. To distract my thoughts, I thought of happy times like when father bought my first pair of ice skates and patiently taught me to ice skate. We laughed a lot during those first attempts until I learned to find my balance. I also remembered the snowball fights we children had with Father in back of the house and Mother's concern that we would catch a cold whenever we came home with ruddy cheeks.

By midday, the handcart felt very heavy, and I was not even halfway to Malomeřice. I made several stops the last few kilometers. Finally, I saw the camp, an old detention center left over from the Nazi era that had not been dismantled after the war; it only changed owners and occupants. Remembering the stories Father had told Mother and me about the mistreatment of prisoners during the Nazi occupation, I shivered to think of what may have happened here. The camp was surrounded by a ten-foot-high heavy gauge, meshed fence with three rows of barbed wire on top and several lookout towers surrounding it. In the inside yard I noticed a couple dozen metal barracks with tin roofs. By the heavy metal gate there was what appeared to be the administration building with an armed guard in front of it. The camp looked very cold and uninviting. I dreaded the thought of going in there but could not go back; there was nowhere else for me to go.

I took a deep breath and headed for the building that had a big stop sign in front of it. As I approached the gate, I saw my parents in the distance crossing the yard, coming towards me. Oh, thank God they were here. Nothing else mattered now.

The guard at the gate told my parents to stay back, pointing for me to go first to the administration office. The formality of processing my papers there went smoothly. I was a minor and had no property, money, or jewelry to relinquish and was soon allowed to pass with all my belongings in tow. It had been a year since I had seen my parents but it seemed much longer. Both appeared malnourished. Father's face was very pale; his eyes showed distress and reflected the pain he had witnessed in captivity. Mother's usually rosy cheeks were pasty and her hair had turned gray. In her smile, I saw a sign of sadness, and her eyes no longer had the twinkle that I remembered enjoying as a child. We hugged for a long time. It was good to see them again and have them close. All three of us started talking at the same time; we had a lot to say. Father wondered how I managed to transport the big sack. When he saw the handcart, he marveled that it still worked. Both he and Mother were relieved to have some of their possessions back.

We were allowed to sit outside one of the barracks on some wooden benches and talk. Our first topic was our next destination—West Germany, which was heavily damaged from the war, its economy in ruins. Would we be able to find work? How would the West Germans treat us? We wondered about Erwin and Lilli and dared to hope that they were alive and safe.

Mother then showed me where I would be sleeping: Barrack #8, which had no regular beds with mattresses and pillows—only multiple sets of three-layered bunks made of wooden slats. Each set of three was separated by a narrow walkway from the next set. Mother said that I was assigned to the one next to her on the top row. As I climbed up, I noticed that all of bunks were filled with straw and had a rancid, dusty odor. I hoped that I would be tired enough every night to fall asleep without noticing the smell or the dust.

In the center of the barrack were long, narrow tables and open back benches with barely enough room to pass between them and the cubicles. I tried to imagine how crowded these barracks must be when full of women. Men were housed in different barracks across the yard.

It was not long before I saw the units fill up with women as they returned from their work detail, weeding the camp vegetable garden. Rain had fallen the day before; that made outside work almost impossible. As the women entered the yard, mud fell from their shoes and clothing. At one of the cold-water spigots behind one of the barracks, they cleaned up the best they could before entering the barrack. Privacy was nonexistent and the smell from their wet and dirty clothing in the hot barrack was overwhelming. I was hoping that we did not have to stay in the camp too long.

At about 7:00 p.m., we lined up for food outside the barracks where a truck with two large metal containers was parked. As the drivers lifted the lids to the kettles, the smell of food drifted towards me. I had not eaten all day and was looking forward to a meal. Along with a slice of dark rye bread, we were served a scoop full of thick, spicy potato stew. It almost choked me and I had to take a big bite of bread to relieve the hot, peppery taste from my mouth. I did not complain. I was hungry.

Later that evening, I climbed up the makeshift ladder into my cubicle for some rest. It had been a long day and I fell asleep almost immediately.

Something woke me up early the next morning. I tried to open my eyes but was unable to; they were swollen shut. I called out to Mother, who after taking one look at me, cried, "My daughter needs help!" I was feverish and swollen from head to toe with bed bug bites. Several women rushed me to the infirmary. Treatment was minimal but I was grateful for any relief.

The following day I saw two men from the International Red Cross come through the infirmary with the camp's Czech officer for what seemed like an inspection tour. Was their visit a coincidence or had someone summoned them? I could not hear everything they were saying as they passed my cot, but I did understand what one Red Cross official said. Pointing to me, he told the camp officer to fumigate all of the barracks and then listed the camp's other health hazards. There were plenty. The night before, I had noticed that there was a pump next to the barrack that also served as a latrine. Women filled their buckets with cold water and then they took turns, without soap, washing the dust from their hands and faces.

The day I was released from the infirmary, I noticed some changes. The food was palatable and the barracks had been thoroughly fumigated. Even so, I dreaded the prospect of sleeping in the place that had sent me to the infirmary.

Several weeks had passed when we received word that our departure date had arrived. One day in early June of 1946 we were told to gather our belongings and meet outside our barracks by six a.m. the next day.

Although I was glad to get out of the camp, the fear of the unknown set in once again. Uncertainty had surrounded me so often during the past few years that I had become numb to the prospect of finding stability in my life. As I gathered my belongings, I was wondering how long it would take, if at all, to once again find a place I could call home.

Brno's Cathedral of St. Peter and Paul[7]

---

7 JUAN RAMON RODRIGUEZ SOSA / el coleccionista de instantes available under Creative Commons attribution-share alike license

92

A Final Act of Intimidation

EARLY THE NEXT MORNING, we gathered outside the barracks and as the guards called our names, we lined up in alphabetical order. As we spoke to some of the people in line, each had a different story about how they had missed being on the Brno Death March the year before. With the exception of Mother and me, none of the others we spoke to had experienced the march. We all knew plenty who had marched but had not returned. After we were all accounted for, the guards opened the large, heavy gates and escorted us to the freight depot, only a short distance away. We were ready for the journey.

Before we were assigned to one of the two-dozen boxcars waiting on the tracks, government officials again thoroughly examined our papers just as they had the day we arrived at the camp. The boxcars reminded me of cattle cars, which have no windows—just one small opening on each end for the animals to get air. Our car was towards the end of the train, and Father was one of only a few able men who could help the women and children get aboard the car with all their boxes and bags. Before leaving the depot several hours later, the guards positioned themselves, one on top of each car, as escorts for the journey. Did they think someone would want to "escape?" Where would we go? By now we had no sense of belonging to a country that had once been dear to us. This last measure of posting armed guards to watch over us was their final act of intimidation and a demonstration of power over us.

Our final instructions were to keep the doors closed while we rode through the stations. Only when the train stopped could we get off to relieve ourselves. To withstand the foul odor in our car, we took turns sitting on the luggage, packed almost to the ceiling on both ends of the car, in order to rest our feet and take in the fresh air that blew in through the small openings. I could not tell whether the odor came from the animals that had recently stood where we were now or from our own weary, unwashed bodies. Once we left the station, we opened the doors. Some of us sat with our feet hanging on the outside, giving those inside the car more room. Conditions were still crowded, but we made do. Father estimated our trip would last two days. The constant bouncing along the tracks made for a very uncomfortable, exhausting ride, but if Father's estimation of our travel was correct, Mother and I thought we could bear it.

No one spoke. As I watched the landscape of my homeland pass by, I wondered what might lie ahead. At one of the villages we passed, Father saw a station name that indicated we were heading towards Bavaria, the southeastern part of Germany. Two days passed and then another; we were still not at the border. Finally, on the fourth day, tired, dirty, and starving, we reached Germany- and none too soon, as some of our fellow passengers were failing from lack of water and food.

Father was right in one of his predictions: we did cross the border into Bavaria. As the train slowed down, everyone was excited and cheered. We tore off the white armbands we had to wear while in Czechoslovakia and threw them into the nearby fields. Our first act of freedom felt liberating! A sigh of relief escaped everyone's lips.

At the border checkpoint, our escort guards came down from their posts. In a small ceremony, a contingent of American soldiers in dress uniforms officially took over the responsibility for the train. At first, we were cautiously optimistic. However, when one of the American officers welcomed us into the Federal Republic of West Germany, everyone clapped. In broken but understandable German, one of the soldiers announced that our first stop was a documentation checkpoint where we would be interviewed, following which everyone would take showers, eat, and then spend the night in military barracks. Many of us applauded and cheered. At last, we were being treated like humans!

After our first night on German soil, we were separated into smaller groups according to our destination and assigned to buses that would take us to our new homes. Our group filled two buses that headed into the Bavarian countryside. The thought of being free and in a democratic country was thrilling and overwhelming. No longer did I have to avoid people looking at me with my white armband, afraid of being recognized as German.

I learned about democracy in school during Hitler's regime. One teacher in fourth grade, a staunch Nazi loyalist, told us that in such a government everything was controlled by rich Jews who exploited the working class for their own selfish gains. As children, we accepted this statement; consulting a history book for an explanation would not have helped. Hitler's propaganda was pervasive, both inside and outside the classroom. During the four-day train ride west, Father, in anticipation of the changes that he hoped would lie ahead, had explained to me the ideological differences between a dictatorship and a democratic government. I was looking forward to experiencing the liberties he spoke of like listening to unbiased commentaries on the radio and reading newspapers that reported the truth. During the interviews at the border, for the first time since the start of the war in 1939, we were encouraged to speak openly about the past year under the Communists and the years before under the Nazis. Was this invitation to speak freely a taste of democracy? I was eager to experience the concept.

After traveling several hours, our two buses, which carried all of our belongings as well as sixty army cots issued to us by the American army, stopped in a small village surrounded by rolling farmland and patches of woods. We could see farmers in their fields harvesting hay and planting winter wheat. When the buses came to a stop in front of a small restaurant and an equally small grocery store, it looked as though these were the only two businesses in the village, other than the post office at the end of the road.

Once we stepped off the buses, the mayor of this tiny village welcomed us. Pointing to the second floor of the restaurant, he said, "You will be staying here in our recreation hall on your army cots until arrangements with the farmers can be made for more permanent housing. To get you started in your new life, you will receive new ID cards, ration coupons, and 30 DM Deutsche Mark (German Marks) per person." With the help of some men from the village, we carried our belongings and the cots to our temporary living quarters. When laid out in the small recreational hall, the cots looked like sardines in a can. There was no storage space, tables or chairs to sit on, and no showers—only the standard facilities of a country restaurant, one for men and one for women. We were told that the village had only twenty-six properties and small farms scattered in the surrounding area, making a total of forty-one homesteads in the village— quite a contrast for me who had grown up in a city of three hundred and fifty thousand inhabitants.

The following day Mother and I started canvassing the nearby farms for day work. Father had already found a job. The day we arrived, he met the local blacksmith, who gave him a part-time job in his shop. The women in each household not only worked in the fields but also tended to household chores, so we thought there would be plenty of work left to be done, like washing clothes, mopping floors and cooking meals. We were right, but "refugees," as we were called, were known to be willing to work from dawn until nightfall for as little as a meal for themselves and their families. We knew we could expect no more. Mother and I found one of the farms in the village with plenty of work to be done. The farmer's wife had her hands full. Besides working in the fields and looking after her household, her father was sick with tuberculosis. We did not worry about getting infected; we needed to work. Our job was to sanitize the house as well as do standard housecleaning. We worked hard and were grateful for our wages: a couple of eggs and a pitcher of milk or homemade bread to take home at the end of a full day.

After a month or so, we were assigned to a farm about a half an hour away where a farmer had relinquished his main living space for Father, Mother, and me. The government asked all households to voluntarily give up some of their living space without compensation to the millions of refugees from Eastern Europe. There were five million of us trying to find new roots in a bombed-out, economically ruined West Germany. Many farmers in the area shared their space reluctantly and hoped that they could come out ahead with the free labor they could get in return. Others considered us intruders and did not welcome us. A few were polite but reserved. Although we spoke the same language, we were foreigners to them; we did not belong. We were assigned to live in house number 38- the Wachbergers' farm. When we arrived with our belongings and the three cots, Mrs. Wachberger introduced herself and led us to our living quarters—their main living room. It was empty, with no chairs to sit on and no table to eat off of. On the side of the room close to the kitchen door was a glaze-tiled wood-burning stove without a cooking surface. Its only function was to keep their living room warm in the winter.

When she saw mother's bewildered look, she explained that the opening to the stove was in the kitchen where the alcove for the wood was also located. "You can use our kitchen stove for your cooking and the sink to wash your dishes," she added. As we walked into the kitchen, I saw a six-by-four-foot stove and a large triple sink by the back window. To the right of it was a large eating area with benches and chairs to accommodate about twelve people; to the left of it was the family's sitting area. Next to the door going into our room was the furnace door and the alcove for the wood to service our tile stove.

Although she told us that we could use her kitchen, her offer did not sound sincere. We did not want to impose on the family even further by using their facilities and interfering with their family routine. We knew it was best to keep to ourselves. We walked back to our room and settled in as best we could. Our clothes stayed in a large bag, which we placed in one corner on the floor. We used a large cardboard box as a table. By day our cots were chairs. None of us complained; we had a roof over our heads.

During the first few days, any attempt on our part to be considerate and helpful was greeted with cold indifference. A week after our arrival Mother and I approached the farmer and asked whether we could work for our meals. We hoped that helping on the farm would not only provide our food, but also facilitate a pleasant relationship between our two families. The Wachbergers smiled for the first time since our arrival and agreed.

Theirs was one of the larger farms in the area—with fifteen cows, eight horses, a dozen pigs and geese, and chickens too numerous to count. Hundreds of acres of fields, pasture, and woods spread as far as the eye could see. On the backside of the property were an apple orchard and several acres of other fruit trees. They also grew hops, a very lucrative crop perfectly suited to the climate. Breweries in Bavaria welcomed the availability of hops so close to their plants.

The farmer, his wife, and their two teenaged children did most of the work in the fields. During harvest time, however, they hired help from other farms until all the crops in the area were under roof. All the farms were self-sustaining but for an occasional trip to the village store for some items they did not produce themselves. The Wachberger's farm was isolated from the rest. The only contact they had with the outside world was a small weekly newspaper. A mail truck that came through once a day was the only sign of life beyond this tiny rural community. Current world events were too far away and disconnected from their daily life to be of any importance.

Sunday was set aside for church attendance and rest. The nearest church in this all-Catholic part of Bavaria was about four miles away. There was no public transportation and none of the farmers could afford the luxury of a car, so we walked. We could hear the bells ringing once we were halfway there, reminding everyone to hurry to get there on time. Women sat on one side of the aisle, men on the other, and all youth sat in the balcony. The two-hour mass was given in Latin.

The first time I knelt on wooden boards for the full service, I almost fainted. Years of malnutrition had caught up with me, but the farmers did not understand. They did not know the toll the last three years had on displaced Germans, and they were wedded to their traditions. When I asked whether I could place a cushion on the kneeling board, the farmer's wife said, "Absolutely not." On Sunday mornings I often pretended I was sick in order to stay home and not embarrass myself by fainting in church, but staying home without giving a reason would mean condemnation from the parishioners. On occasion, I left the service early because I felt weak and lightheaded. As I walked down the aisle and out the door, I could hear the youth in the upper balcony whispering and giggling. On many occasions I heard them say, "I wonder what Margit was 'up to' last night." Oh, how I missed Uncle Hugo's church, where no outside influences had interfered with my communion with God. His was a small, simple chapel with only a few wooden benches and stone-tiled floors that have felt many footsteps over hundreds of years. Its windows and walls emanated peace and warmth and touched the spirits of those who entered. In this Bavarian country church so far from home, I did not feel a welcoming warmth nor feel the loving spirit I so desperately longed for.

I was beginning to dislike our new homeland and everything in it. Whenever I complained, Father told me to be patient. "The war has left everything in chaos," he explained. "It will take time for German cities to rebuild. But don't worry, they will and we will relocate into a city where we can create a new life." In the meantime, with the help from the mayor's office, Father found a job near Augsburg, where the clearing of rubble from the reconstruction of several factories had begun. Though he had enjoyed the blacksmithing job in the village, it had been only part time. During the week, he shared a room in Augsburg with another worker and on weekends he came home. The manual labor proved too taxing for my fifty-four year old father. The year of captivity after the war had compromised his health. Whenever he came home on the weekends for rest and clean clothing, I could see the price he had to pay; he had lost weight, his cheeks were hollow, and his shoulders drooped.

Mother and I continued to work on the farm. She helped Mrs. Wachberger with her household chores and I, though inexperienced and underfed, became a valuable asset on the farm. I cleaned their horse stables, milked their cows, and planted as well as harvested their crops. During harvest time, I learned to drive the team of horses that brought the loaded wagons to the farm, helped unload the crops, and then drove the team back into the fields for another load. I pumped water from the well and hauled it in buckets to whoever needed it. At times, night fell before we were done with our assigned chores. The farm had no electricity, so we worked in the dark by kerosene lamps, sometimes rising as early as four in the morning and not finishing until eleven at night. With time, I adapted to the hard work and primitive conditions.

Mother, on the other hand, was perpetually tired and short of breath. She also suffered from swollen feet and legs. When we consulted a doctor in town, he suggested that she stop working because she was developing heart problems. We could not afford to consult a heart specialist or buy better medication than what the doctor had given her, so we took all the precautionary measures we could for her. When we told the farmer about her condition, he acknowledged our situation, but beyond that showed little understanding or sympathy. At first, she continued doing work that allowed her to sit down, but soon that too became increasingly difficult. She was getting too weak to work and was preoccupied with her two older children. She had not seen them since Christmas of 1943, and our last correspondence from them had reached us in March of 1945. Their present locations were unknown to us.

Since our arrival in Germany, we had sought the addresses of agencies that reunited military personnel with their displaced families. There were millions of them from all across Europe and the International Red Cross had their hands full. On my day off from work I corresponded with the Red Cross, asking for their help in locating Erwin and Lilli and our lost family friend Steffi, whom we had not heard from since the Russian occupation of Brno.

By mid-August, we received a letter from Lilli. Oh, what joy and relief it brought us. I could see a change in Mother's countenance and energy level; she smiled more often and seemed to take more interest in daily activities. Lilli wrote about how she had made her way through the Russian and American lines to West Germany. She was only four hours away by train, and as soon as she had an answer from us, she would come see us. We could hardly wait for Father to come home that weekend to tell him the good news. I wrote a short note to Lilli telling her that we were anxiously expecting her and that we would talk about everything else in person. I could not get my letter to the post office fast enough!

A week later, we received word of her arrival. I took the postal truck to town and asked the driver to reserve two seats for my return trip. He was just as excited as I was that my sister and I would be reunited, after four long years. When I met her at the train station, I could see that the war had left its mark on her features as well; she was gaunt and her once youthful forehead now had fine lines. But she was alive, and I was happy to see her again! She spent the whole month of August with us, during which time Mother tended to our small vegetable garden and picked wildflowers for our room. It was good to see her smiling and being active again.

Lilli told us of her experiences during the last days of war: "When our RAD unit in the eastern part of Germany realized that we were going to be captured by the Russians, we took refuge on a Red Cross train that was transporting injured German soldiers heading towards the interior of Germany. Because the Red Cross was a non-combat unit, putting on their nurses' uniforms helped us feel relatively safe. As the train approached one of the rivers in western Germany, however, we realized that American forces were on the other side."

Alarmed, Mother asked, "What did you do?" Lilli continued, "There was no turning back. We were captured by the American Army on May 9, 1945, the day after German capitulation. After our release to Heilbronn, West Germany, I soon found a teaching job. I was lucky." When she asked about Erwin and Steffi, we could not tell her any news. The Red Cross had not yet found them.

With school starting in September, Lilli had to go back to Heilbronn. She promised to visit us as often as possible. We looked forward to writing and sending each other care packages. We needed goods from the city and she wanted fresh produce from our garden. Lilli's stay with us and our subsequent exchange of care packages strengthened Mother's spirit and gave me hope that her health would improve. It did—but not for long.

The Wachberger's farm in Bavaria, our first living quarters
in West Germany

A Joyous Reunion

As WINTER APPROACHED, Father was not able to come home every weekend due to inclement weather. With the colder weather came another concern: keeping Mother warm. Our room and the kitchen were the only heated spaces on the farm, and we were responsible for providing our own wood. On my days off, weather permitting, I went into the woods nearby to collect fallen tree branches, break them into two-foot-long pieces, and pile them along the outside wall of the farmer's barn. By the first snowfall in November, we had enough for the winter. Even so, Mother's condition worsened. By January she was confined to her bed.

One day in early February, after coming home from getting some staple groceries in the village, I noticed that our room was cold and that Mother was shivering under her blankets. The stove tiling was cold and when I went into the kitchen to check the stove opening, I saw that someone had poured water into it. I was outraged.

During the few months we had been there, we knew the Wachbergers did not like our living in their home, and at times they had let us feel it. During harvest time, the farmer had tried to provoke me by sending me into the hayloft to distribute bales of hay more evenly, knowing that I had a severe sunburn and my skin was sensitive. However, taking his frustration out on Mother was too much for me to tolerate without a response.

That evening, after the farmer came home from working in the nearby woods, I told him that we did not choose to be there and suggested that he let his anger and frustration out on the government, not a defenseless, sick woman. He claimed not to know anything about what had happened; I came short of calling him a liar. I rekindled the fire but it took about an hour for the room to get warm again.

I did not tell Mother of my confrontation with the farmer, but she sensed what had happened. That night, as well as many other nights, I heard her crying and praying, asking God, "Why is my life filled with so much pain? What did I do to deserve such a heavy load?" Then she asked Him not to let her die in this country. She told Him that she would like to be buried at home and to have her three children reunited with her and Father. I could not hold back my tears—not just because of her anguish, but because of mine. I lay on my cot on the other side of the room, hoping she would not notice that I had overheard her prayer. Then I silently added my own prayer that God would lead us out of this misery.

A few weeks later, again, someone extinguished the fire in the stove, and a few weeks after that, it happened again. By then I was resigned to the fact that this was our lot and silently went and rekindled the fire. There was nothing else I could do. I was hoping for an early spring.

With spring came plowing, sewing, and planting. I came home at dusk exhausted, but at least I did not have to worry about Mother being cold. We left the windows open so the sun could warm the room. Mother showed a little improvement. On warm days she sat on the front steps and read Lilli's letters over and over again. They were a great comfort to her.

One day in June a letter came from Steffi. I lovingly called her my second mother (Mutti). I told her the stirrings of my heart, just as I had once told Uncle Hugo. Steffi knew things about me that my parents did not. Shortly after her husband passed away and my parents befriended her, Mother sent me to her house with a freshly baked cake for her birthday. Steffi lived only a block from our apartment building and when she asked me to sit down and tell her all about me, I felt immediately drawn to her. When she told me that she had always wanted a little girl and that I could come any time, our friendship grew. I had last seen her when Mother and I evacuated our home, shortly before the Russians occupied Brno.

Steffi wrote that the Red Cross, in response to our inquiry about her, had found her in West Germany. Though she had asked them to search for us, she had not received an answer. She said that she was living and working on an isolated farm in lower Bavaria, not far from us. I was so happy to hear that she was well. In my answer, I told her of our circumstances and invited her to come see us if she was financially able. She answered that she would come in the fall. I so looked forward to her visit.

One day in July, on my way home from my weekly walk to the village to retrieve the mail, I stopped by the roadside to talk to one of the farm workers, when I noticed someone following me at a distance. Everyone who lived in the area knew one another well, so I was surprised I did not recognize the person behind me. As he came closer, though, I again looked in his direction. It was Erwin!

Oh, what a surprise! I ran towards him and held him close. It had been four tumultuous years since we had last seen each other. Oh, how wonderful it was to know that he too had come through the war alive and unscathed. Mother's prayer had been answered; we all had survived!

As we walked towards the farm, I told him of Mother's condition. We decided that he would wait outside while I prepared her for his arrival. I entered the room, put my arms around her, and told her that I had good news for her. Right away she said, "You have news about Erwin? Is he alive?" Then I asked her to be strong, "Yes, he is alive," I said, nodding my head and smiling, "Waiting outside to see you!"

She started trembling and crying. The door opened and Erwin came in. Mother was visibly shaken; I had to hold her in order to keep her from falling out of the chair. I had never seen her more excited! The three of us talked until midnight.

The following day, we sent postcards to Lilli and Steffi, telling them the good news. We could not notify Father by mail because he was coming home the next day. When Father arrived for his week-end's rest and found Erwin there, he looked twice before he recognized the tall man standing in the door with a big grin on his face. Erwin had grown to a man in the four years since we had last seen him. Father's face lit. It was wonderful to see my parents happy! All their children were alive and well! What a blessing!

Our reunion definitely called for a celebration. After church on Sunday, I made some dumplings with flour I had saved up and a chicken that I purchased from a nearby farmer. The finishing touches of gravy and fresh vegetables from the garden made a celebratory feast. We had a great homecoming, all sitting under one of the shade trees on the farm, laughing, reminiscing, and enjoying a good meal. Only Lilli was missing. She was not able to join us on such short notice but sent us a card promising to come see us soon.

After a week of resting, catching up, and discussing future plans, Erwin decided to stay on the farm for a while. He approached the farmer about helping with that year's harvest in exchange for room and board. The farmer readily agreed and Erwin settled in. From then on I noticed a slight change in the farmer's attitude towards us. Was it because he now had an adult male, besides his own two teenaged sons, to help with the heavy work and this year's harvest? I did not know, but we were grateful for even the slightest improvement in our relationship.

Early one day in August, as we started out into the fields, Mother called out to me. She sounded panicked. I rushed back into the house and noticed she was having difficulty breathing; her face was very pale. I called Erwin and asked him to take the bicycle to the neighboring farm where a doctor was spending the night with relatives. Upon my bidding, Erwin asked the doctor to come and look at mother. The doctor came right away, took one look at her, and told us that time was of the essence: she needed immediate attention. They loaded her onto his buggy to take her to the city hospital. Erwin went along.

Instead of working in the fields that day, I walked to the village post office to send a telegram to Father and Lilli about Mother. I asked the postmaster to send his son by bicycle if Erwin called from the hospital. He said he would, but no word came. It was close to midnight when Erwin came home. He explained that though Mother had received good care, her condition was very grave. In fact, she would likely die in the next few days. He agreed to take me to see her the next day on the postal bus. I told him, that I had sent a telegram to Father and Lilli and that I was expecting them to arrive in a day or so.

All of us got to see and talk to her one more time before she closed her eyes for the last time on August 10, 1948. Mother passed away the day after Lilli arrived. I believe that Mother waited to make sure that her family was together once again before leaving us. During my final visit with her, she told me that she would not have made it this far, had I not been with her during and after the war. She told me of her concern about my future, and then, as if seeing a vision, said that I would cross many waters and settle in a country far away; she asked me to be good and strong, and to pray for her. Her voice was weak, at times only a whisper. I had to lean forward, close to her face to hear her. I gently held her in my arms. I was unable to say the many things that I had wanted to tell her since she had told me, in the Peterka family's basement, that I was an unwanted child. I just nodded my head, assuring her I would do as she had asked. I did not want to let go of her and yet, my time was up. Today, looking back, I know that God had a purpose for me to be born under such circumstances and I am grateful for that knowledge. His plan, however, was not revealed to me until nearly thirty years later.

The next person to see Mother was Erwin, followed by Lilli. Father came last. As he came out of her room, he was crying—something I had never seen before. He told us that she had died in his arms. Father had loved her deeply; she would have wanted to die in his arms.

We were all grateful when Lilli decided to take a leave from school to look after everyone and plan the funeral. Arrangements had to be made with the local priest regarding the mass, a burial plot had to be secured, and all the paperwork had to be completed. Father was glad for her help.

Local tradition deemed that we wear black clothing for one full year after a close family member had passed away. We knew this would create a problem for me since I had no black clothes. The wife of a neighboring farmer donated some rough homespun material that she had dyed black and another lady made me a dress from it for the funeral. With the ration coupons we received after arriving in Bavaria, I was able to buy a pair of lightweight shoes that I knew would not hold up on the country roads for too long, but wearing my army boots was out of the question. The day before the funeral, I tried on the homemade black burlap dress. It was a perfect fit, but I was allergic to the material. I dreaded the thought of walking in the funeral procession on a hot August day. Not to insult the generosity of the women in the neighborhood, I decided to wear the black dress for the funeral.

Lilli was in a similar predicament; she also did not have a dress for the funeral that would meet the parishioner's approval. However, she was not worried about what the townspeople would say if she violated the local customs because after the service, she would never see them again. Only a handful of people attended the short church and gravesite service, mostly fellow refugees and a few farmers' wives, including ours.

We laid Mother to rest, not in her home country, a wish she so often prayed for, but at least in a free country where we could come and visit often. She was buried in a single grave close to the brick wall of the small cemetery that surrounded the church. A shady spot—she would have liked it. The following Sunday, I went to visit the gravesite and attend church.

The rash that had developed on my back and arms from wearing the burlap dress was still bright red, so I wore a blue dress, the only one I owned besides my working clothes. As I entered the church, I noticed heads turning and then heard whispering coming from the balcony above. I did not care about not following their rules or worry about fainting from kneeling on the wooden boards. For the first time, I stayed seated and was able to sit through the service without feeling sick.

Out of respect for and in memory of my Mother, I attended services and visited her grave every Sunday for a few months. Despite people's reactions, I wore my blue dress. I carried my sorrow in my heart; there was no need to display it openly for all to see by wearing black clothing. I was not surprised when my decision left me shunned by the community. But I couldn't concentrate on my prayers during church services; my utterances to God became empty words. I felt myself slowly drifting spiritually away from the church and the beliefs I had formed since sitting by Uncle Hugo's side.

A few months passed. Erwin joined Father in Augsburg on a construction site, coming home only for the weekends to rest and get clean clothing. I was by myself, working long hours. Then a letter from Steffi came. She was sorry about not being able to attend Mother's funeral and wrote that she could come to see us for a week in September. I so looked forward to finally having someone to talk to. On the day of her arrival, I took the postal truck to the train station. Oh, how good it was to see her again after four long years. Like all refugees, Steffi too showed the signs of her past experiences etched in her face. Although she was only in her forties, her brown hair showed grey streaks, her hands had calluses from hard farm work, and her clothes were worn. So much had happened since I had last seen her that I knew it would take us the whole week to catch up. On our way home in the postal truck, I learned about her solo escape and flight across the Czech border into Germany with only the clothes on her back.

I told her what had happened since Mother's passing, including my relentless nightmares of being pursued by Russian soldiers and being pressed by Czech mobs that chased me and threatened to kill me. On occasions, I dreamed that I was killed and buried alive—unable to die. Every time this happened, I woke up with cold perspiration all over my body. This had been going on since we had left home, but I had chosen not to tell Mother. I did not want to give her something else to worry about.

Steffi was a good listener. She knew that my heart was full and needed an outlet. I told her that since Mother died, my Sunday church visits had been not as spiritual as they had been in my early years. I had kept my faith throughout a horrible war and the persecution that followed—but now my faith was spent. I explained, "Steffi, I am losing my faith because people at church ridicule me for not being able to kneel during Mass without fainting, and because I do not feel close to God when I pray. I feel it is time to leave the Catholic Church for good."

She put her arms around me, trying to console me. I continued, "As a child, Uncle Hugo taught me how to pray and helped me build my faith. I did not fully understand the doctrine of the Trinity or the Latin Sunday Service, but I did believe in God, Jesus Christ, and the Holy Ghost. I felt close to God then, but now it seems that the God I knew has deserted me. He has taken everything that I ever loved—my childhood, my country, and now my mother. And I can't find any answers. I no longer feel loved by God."

When I looked up at Steffi, I could see that she was ready to hear anything I wanted to say. I told her I did not know where to turn. The people who attended the community church had alienated me. They did not know the pain I carried in my heart and even if they did, they did not care. Relieved to give words to my pain and disappointment, I finally said, "This is too much to bear. A loving God would not let things like this happen."

Steffi told me that it was not God who had let me down. "The war and its terrible aftermath have torn away your sense of intimacy with your Heavenly Father. And now, after all the atrocities of war, you believe it is only the cruel rebuffs at church that have broken your spirit." Although I listened to her intently, I could not dismiss the bitterness I felt.

"Let time heal your wounds," Steffi continued, "Perhaps finding another church will help you find His presence, the warmth and comfort, the assurance of His love—again." She smiled at me as she put her arms around my shoulders and kissed my cheeks.

The postal truck had almost reached our destination when I told her that since Mother's death, Father spent most Saturdays at the local beer hall. I understood his pain, but did not know how to help him. Before I could continue, Steffi said, "Would you like me to move here and help you?" "Oh, yes," I said quickly, fearing she might change her mind.

When Father and Erwin came home for the weekend, we had a wonderful reunion with Steffi and talked about her relocating. Father and Erwin had taken a few extra days off work so we could visit a little longer and by the end of Steffi's time with us, she and Father decided to get married. This welcome news was not really a surprise; they had known each other for many years and were both alone. I was delighted to have her join the family. Out of respect to my mother and local customs they waited until the following summer to marry. I knew Mother would approve of this union, as she and Steffi had been very close.

There was a lot to prepare and get ready for in the meantime. Telling Steffi goodbye at the train station this time was a happy occasion, for I knew that the next time I saw her would be to help her settle in for good. Soon, Erwin moved to Augsburg for a job that would bring him enough money to rent a room from a family there; thankfully, he came to visit every other month and on long holiday weekends.

I was able to see Steffi sooner than we thought possible. A neighbor's mother had recently passed away and when her son heard of Steffi's relocating, he offered his mother's cottage to my Father in exchange for watching their children- infant twins and a three-year old. Steffi wrote that she was delighted with the arrangement and then made her own suggestion for me: that I ask Lilli to find me a job in Heilbronn. I was too young, she wrote, to be isolated on a farm where there was no future for me. "Move to the city," she urged, "to pursue your education and develop your talents." During her first short visit, she had observed that I had nothing in common with the young people in our small agricultural community. Except for an occasional church party or dance I attended, I had no social life. There were also no opportunities for me to develop my cultural interests and other than reading an old book that our farmer's children had lying on a shelf, there was nothing to stimulate my mind.

Perhaps she also realized that with Mother's passing, she would be asked, at times, to play a double role—that of a friend and substitute mother. Though childless, she fell into this role with grace and ease. We came from different religious traditions, I Catholic and she Protestant, but I respected her advice and wisdom in all matters, including spiritual ones.

I did write Lilli, who promised to try to find something. I knew it would be difficult as the country was only slowly getting back on its feet and the Heilbronn business district had been leveled during the war. This small city at the foot of the Neckar River lay nestled in the hills of Würtemberg's wine region. There were not many businesses open yet, and Lilli lived in a one-bedroom apartment on the outskirts of town, teaching a class of sixth graders. I was hoping that through her contact with her students' parents, she could find something suitable for me.

Anticipating a change in my life, I worked even harder on my chores at the farm. Winter passed and with the longer, sunny days came planting, which I enjoyed. Time went by quickly. Lilli wrote that she was still looking for the right opportunity for me and let us know that she was getting married in November, and would definitely attend Father's and Steffi's wedding in September. Her announcement of marriage came as a surprise to us; we had not known that she was dating anyone and we looked forward to meeting this new member to the family.

With the harvest under roof and our move to the neighboring farm completed by early September, a letter came from Lilli that she had found me a job. Since I had no training and needed a place to live as well, she thought a job as a live-in housekeeper would be best. She had met the parents of one of her students. When they expressed a need for someone to keep their newly rebuilt home clean, she urged them to hire me. The family worked and lived above their own bakery and coffee shop in town. I could start in the fall. I thought it was a wonderful opportunity to get off the farm, so I accepted the position.

Soon after Steffi arrived with her belongings, Erwin came for a couple of days to help us move from the Wachberger farm to the neighboring Steinemann farm where we felt like welcomed guests rather than an imposition. We were looking forward to living in a friendlier atmosphere. What did it matter that the living quarters were smaller? Soon after the move, on September 16, 1949, in a small, simple ceremony, Father and Steffi were married.

Afterwards, Lilli and I helped Steffi and Father get settled in their new living space. Farmer Steinemann gave them a small table and some chairs. His wife donated a pair of lace curtains for the windows and a small flower bouquet for the table; it started to look like a home. With Steffi and Father settled, Erwin returned to Augsburg, and Lilli and I boarded the train headed to Heilbronn.

As we said good-bye at the train station, Steffi put her arms around me and whispered, "Keep your faith and promise to look for Him." I nodded and said, "I will. I promise."

The war was behind us and we dared to hope that the years of discrimination were as well. Little did we know that forty years would pass before our family's next reunion.

On December 4, 1944, 282 planes bombed the city of Heilbronn. Within a period of half an hour, over 6,500 people (including 1,000 children) lost their lives. The city of Heilbronn was still in ruins when I arrived three years later to find a job and start a new life.

CHAPTER TWELVE

Crossing the Atlantic to a New Life

WHEN LILLI AND I boarded the train from Bavaria to the once beautiful wine country of Württemberg, shell holes still dotted the landscape. Where large industrial plants once stood, only mounts of rubble, twisted steel beams and blocks of concrete remained. As the train passed through larger cities, we could see new businesses and homes emerging from the rubble. Heilbronn was no different, but I knew it would someday, like the rest of the country, rise from the ashes of the war.

With my small suitcase in hand, I navigated through the streets dotted with the occasional new buildings—among them the bakery and home of my new employers, Mr. and Mrs. Roman. Over the new store's entrance hung a temporary sign: Roman's Bakery and Café. Lilli introduced me to the couple and their young daughter Erika. "We hope you will like it here," Mrs. Roman said with a big smile. She showed me around the house and took me to my room in the loft. "We have worked hard rebuilding our business and living space, and would hope that as you help us keep it clean and do the laundry for the café, you will also feel at home," she explained. "Lilli has told us that you were expelled from your home and that you, like all of us, look forward to a new start." Relieved and thankful to have landed with such a pleasant family, I slept well that night.

With the connections Lilli and the Romans had in the local school system, I was able to attend evening classes at a popular adult education program so that I could complete my high school education, which had been interrupted during the last year of the war. Although we met in makeshift classrooms, there was a vibrant spirit present. Ready to rebuild their country, young people were eager to learn and develop. Subjects were taught from a politically unbiased point of view and I made good progress in all subjects—particularly in my twentieth century European history class where I discovered how the government-controlled media and press had misled the German population during the war. Learning the truth was sobering and having the freedom to express my opinion was liberating.

While I was catching up with my education, the Marshall Plan, the European Recovery Program was underway. Many of the cities in Germany and other European countries were either in ruin or were greatly damaged. The Marshall Plan provided aid for the economic restructuring of the countries in greatest need. Soon after the Plan was initiated, stores once again displayed merchandise—something we had not seen in years. Business in the bakery increased considerably and Mr. Roman gave me a raise—my first ever! On the farm we had worked only for our room and board, so handling money was new to me. I saved my wages to buy my first new pair of shoes. As I proudly walked out of the shoe store with my treasure in hand, a pair of brown leather pumps with small heels, my thoughts went to my army boots from the Russian lady officer. They had saved my feet and served me well, but that life seemed like it belonged to someone else.

With time, I came to realize that to advance in this new economy, knowledge of the English language was an absolute must. As American occupying forces became part of Germany's landscape, English became the country's second language. I had often heard that the best way to learn a language was to go to the country where it is spoken. So when I heard of a job in London that involved taking care of blind students, I applied and was soon accepted. This all-expense paid position was offered to young women from all over Europe by the British government and its National Institute for the Blind. The Institute helped young adults who had lost their sight in the war adjust to their new lives. Nearly all of the residents were victims of war-related injuries.

There were five girls hired that year: two from Switzerland, one from Finland, one from France, and me. We were each assigned four students. Our first week, we were trained in how to tend to their needs. We taught them how to take care of themselves and how to keep their surroundings clean and orderly.

Sometimes we discussed world events or invited them to play games with us such as checkers or table tennis. During our many discussions, politics and the war came up. Though some of us came from countries that had fought for the Third Reich and two from a neutral country, there was never any tension—just a desire to learn from each other and to process what had happened to us. The two girls from Switzerland were especially eager to listen to our experiences. The blind students, all of whom lived in London during the V-2 attacks towards the end of the war, recounted their horrible experiences of the bombings. One told us that he lost his sight during one of these attacks and after we listened to the details of his terrible ordeal, we decided never to talk about the war again. Instead, we looked for other sources of stimulation and entertainment. All of us enjoyed excursions to downtown London, where we fed the pigeons at Trafalgar Square and enjoyed watching the changing of the guards at Buckingham Palace. We became the students' eyes, describing for them what we saw. In the process we learned to see our surroundings with different eyes.

On my birthday, which is also Queen Elizabeth's, the students and my co-workers decided to surprise me with an IOU to be redeemed in June with an outing to see the "Trooping the Colours," her Majesty's celebrated birthday, full of pageantry and parades at which she inspects her guards. When the day finally came, our student's faces lit up as we described all the colorful uniforms, the horses, Her Royal Highness, and the excited crowd that surrounded us. At one point, the Queen passed us on a beautiful black horse, and a group of small children sitting on the curb jumped to their feet, waving their flags and screaming as loudly as they could. The city was ablaze with excitement. We described it all. Two hours later, after the parade was over and the crowd had dispersed, we walked to a nearby park and enjoyed a picnic lunch. The last surprise was a beautiful cake to celebrate my most memorable twenty-first birthday.

On rainy days, and there are quite a few of those in London, the students taught us how to read in Braille, another activity that brought all of us a lot of joy. We laughed whenever language became a barrier in communicating and after our one-year contract was up, most of us girls knew multiple phrases in each other's languages. I never could master the Finnish expressions, but on the day we left I managed to say to our French co-worker Yvonne: "Au revoir, tu me manqueras," (Goodbye, I am going to miss you).

Saying goodbye to the students was difficult. We had become attuned to their needs and had found great pleasure in caring for them. We always placed the furniture back in the same spot after dusting and cleaning. Each book, article of clothing, and toiletry item had a home in a certain drawer or on a certain shelf. Every inch counted as they navigated through their space. We knew they would miss hearing our footsteps and would have to learn to recognize new ones coming down the hallway every morning. We also knew we would miss them and each other. The day we left London, we five promised to stay in touch with each other and did so for many years. Our friendships had developed while in the service of others.

As I crossed the English Channel back to the continent, I thought of the last conversation I had with my mother. Was the English Channel one of the waters she had predicted I would cross? I had not given it much thought then, but now I think that perhaps it was.

After my time in London, I returned to Germany and took a job as a receptionist at an American army officer's club because I wanted to practice my newly acquired English language skills. Sometimes when I spoke with patrons, they asked whether I was from Britain because of my accent and the expressions I used. Directing patrons to the "lift" instead of the elevator or asking them to "ring" me back instead of calling back was usually followed by corrections and laughter.

During one of these British word exchanges I got to know an American couple, Captain James and Amanda Smith from Tulsa, Oklahoma. I spent many evenings at their home enjoying American food, music, and conversation. They soon became my friends. By the time they were transferred from Germany, I knew that I wanted to go to the United States—not just to visit them, but to live and enjoy the prosperity and freedoms of which they spoke. But I soon learned that my dream of immigrating to the United States would have to wait: there was a quota and the only way to be one of the selected few was to have a qualifying degree or highly desirable technical skills.

I hung onto my dream, worked in the Club, and volunteered for overtime whenever I could to earn the extra money needed to travel across the Atlantic. One day I heard from Johanna, a German colleague from the Club, that Canada's visa quota had not been filled. As she was also eager to go to the United States, she suggested we go together. I leapt at the chance and applied for a visa. Through an acquaintance she found someone in Canada who was willing to sponsor her and later me. Finally, I could leave all the reminders of the past behind and plan a new life. Not so easy, however, was the thought of saying goodbye to my family and friends, not knowing whether I would ever see them again. In early March I took the train to Bavaria, to see Father and Steffi one more time. As the train moved through the countryside, fields were being prepared for planting and memories of my years on the farm came to my mind.

I was glad to leave some of the bitter memories behind but I was happy to see Father and Steffi when I arrived. We had a long and meaningful visit. Father gave me a small St. Christopher charm for my journey, and Steffi and I had a long heart-to-heart talk. I promised her that I would search for that spiritual fulfillment that I could not find when I left Bavaria the first time. "God be with you," she said, as I waved from the train going back to Heilbronn.

Eight months passed before all the documents and correspondence were completed and approved. In late March of 1957, I boarded the MS Berlin and after seven days at sea, I arrived in Halifax, Nova Scotia. The one-thousand-mile train ride from the port to Ottawa took me through the eastern Canadian provinces. Snow and ice covered the vast countryside. The size of the farms that we passed surpassed those in Bavaria many times over. I wondered how many hands and hours it took during the summer months to bring the harvest home. Some fields seemed to reach from one end of the horizon to the other, and as the train rushed by, I wondered how much equipment was necessary to plant and cultivate such enormous areas. It was both overwhelming and liberating to see these wide open fertile fields slip past the train window. Occasionally, we passed a lone farmhouse and I remembered the isolated farm in Bavaria where my parents and I had lived. It now seemed to be part of someone else's life.

When we pulled into the Ottawa train station, Johanna was waiting for me. "It's so good to see you," she exclaimed and immediately filled me in on all of her experiences since her arrival. "Did you know they have Chinese restaurants over here?" Full of enthusiasm, she took me to one within walking distance that she had just discovered. It was an easy sell; I loved it!

Our dream of moving to the United States had now inched a little closer. Only a few days after my arrival, she helped me get a job as an instrument technician at the hospital where she worked.

This type of work was new to me, but I enjoyed the challenge of preparing surgical trays and packages for various operating procedures as well as making certain that everything was sterile and all instruments were accounted for. A couple of days later I settled into a tiny loft apartment within walking distance from Johanna's and soon we were ready to explore the city together. One weekend we visited Niagara Falls; it was a magnificent site! Though the view was far better on our side, we both knew that our dream to move across the bridge and into the United States had not diminished.

I had told Johanna about the rejections and prejudice I had experienced in Bavaria. As we stood next to the rushing falls, with a sweeping motion of her hand, she said, "There is the land where all our dreams and hopes can come true. I hope to find my true love over there." Then she turned to look at me and added, "I hope you can put your past behind you, find new spiritual strength, and feel God's love once again." I put my arms around her and thanked her for her thoughtfulness. It was a memorable moment.

I loved my new job at the hospital and after only six months of working in the operating room, I was offered a training position as an operating room technician. I had worked with instruments and was familiar with sterilization and other procedures, so I immediately signed up for the two-year training course. Halfway through the program, however, I noticed a help wanted ad in the local paper for a full-time housekeeper in a Canadian diplomat's home in Chicago. Though I was enjoying the training and knew I was on track for a well-paid and secure career, I did not hesitate to apply. No matter what the job, I wanted to step on American soil.

Two weeks later, the attorney who handled the applications for the position called to inform me that the family had selected me. He asked me to come to his office the following day. I could hardly believe it! There I was, a foreign-born person, barely a year in North

America, getting a job in the United States! Later, I learned that I had been chosen from over two hundred applicants.

Early the next morning, I went to see Mr. Ashcroft, the attorney. He congratulated me for landing the job, assuring me that I would enjoy working for his longtime friends, Mr. and Mrs. Newman, the Canadian Consul General in Chicago. He also gave me a train ticket to go to the Consulate in Montreal and back, and some spending money. I was on cloud nine, ready for the adventure!

What would normally take months, took less than a day. I was not aware of it at the time, but Mr. Ashcroft paved the way by letting the immigration officials in Montreal know that I was coming. I walked into that office the next day, gave the receptionist my name, and within fifteen minutes walked out with my visa in hand! At the American Embassy close by, a plane ticket and spending money were also waiting for me. The opportunity to move from Canada to the United States had come earlier than expected. I had anticipated filling out dozens of forms and long, long lines, but there I was at the threshold of a new experience, ready to open the door.

On the train ride back to Ottawa I thought of the time when Mother and I were hiding in the bunker of the Peterka home outside Brno, waiting for the Russian soldiers to come and fearing for our lives. Fourteen years has passed since then. Looking at that airline ticket in my hand, I felt greatly blessed. This was to be my first plane flight ever! A dream had come true! I had never imagined entering the United States in such grand style. When I landed in Chicago, I was greeted by a chauffeur who picked up my luggage and took me on an extended ride through the city to the official residence of the Canadian Consul General on Lake Shore Drive.

My new home was a two-story condominium in a high-rise overlooking Lake Michigan. On the lower floor, facing the lake, were a huge living room and dining room; adjacent to them was a pantry and behind that the kitchen, a small office and my living quarters. Other staff, like the chauffeur, a houseman, and a laundry woman, lived outside the residence. Mrs. Newman liked to do her own cooking so there was no cook on staff. Five out of seven days a week we had official functions at the residence. My job was to clean the living quarters and make sure everything was in place for scheduled functions. I laid out the linen; set the tables with silver and china; and arranged the furniture and flowers for all the events.

Mrs. Newman made all the weekly schedules with room layouts and loved preparing all the food herself. Only on rare occasions, such as the reception for the British Royal couple, would she use a caterer. It was in her kitchen that I learned how to prepare various Canadian dishes and hors d'oeuvres. My favorites were her stuffed mushrooms and crispy cheese sticks.

Mrs. Newman often introduced me to her guests, always complimenting me, sometimes affectionately calling me her adopted daughter. From the outset, the Newmans treated me like one of their own, so I had the opportunity to meet many notable people, among them Mayor Richard J. Daley. Before Her Majesty Queen Elizabeth II and the Duke of Edinburgh Prince Philip visited Chicago, British dignitaries planning the Royal visit, dined and held meetings at the Newmans' residence. Two weeks prior to the Royal visit, I was invited by Robert Whyte Mason, the British Consul General, to see to the needs of Canadian Prime Minister's wife while they stayed at the Drake Hotel. I felt greatly honored to stand with other attendants in line of the Drake Hotel as the Royal couple, the Prime Minister and Mrs. Diefenbaker, as well as other dignitaries, arrived and walked through the beautifully decorated lobby. As a token of gratitude, Mrs. Diefenbaker gave me a huge bouquet of four-dozen red roses from her room when she left. A personal note was attached so I could pass security.

With the Newmans' two daughters away at college, one in Canada and the other in Ireland, I somehow filled the void. Many evenings, after the guests had left, Mr. and Mrs. Newman invited me to join them in their big family room to watch television and enjoy ice cream and cookies. It did not take long for me to learn the rules of ice hockey and become an avid fan of the Montreal Canadians. Sundays were set aside for church; the Newmans, devout Christian Scientists, often invited me to join them in their Sunday church attendance and on special occasions I did.

The Newmans believed in and read the Bible and other church-related publications on a regular basis. Although I loved and respected my employers, I did not follow or believe the tenets of their religion. For example, I did not agree with their claim that illness could be overcome only by applying Christian teachings; medical care was prohibited, as were prescription drugs.

Most Sundays I attended a small Presbyterian church just down the street on Michigan Avenue, but I soon discovered that I did not feel happy or spiritually fed there either. Thinking that perhaps it was the social aspect that I was missing, I attended a singles' group the church offered but felt out of place there too. Most of the young people my age were highly educated professionals from prominent families. I was a foreigner without wealth, connections, or a college degree and had a past that haunted me. Was I going to feel out of place and behind the rest of my life? When I shared my feelings with Mrs. Newman, she smiled at me and said, "No, dear. All of life's experiences are lessons the Lord wants you to learn, and He will teach you how to handle them. It will be up to you to accept the teachings. We don't know why some of us have harder lives than others, but in the end, how we handle the challenges is what matters."

I then told her about my strong faith in God as a child and how the war, all the trials that followed, and my mother's death had broken my heart—and my faith. I told her, "When I came to this country, I was hoping to find a church where I could find God again and once again be happy." Mrs. Newman shared with me that as a young adult she had had a near-death experience that turned her life around completely. "Now," she said, "I focus on whatever is God's will and don't worry about the rest. Whenever the Lord chooses for you to find the church and the teachings He has prepared for you, He will guide you to it and give you, just as He has me, blessings in abundance." I thanked her for her encouraging words. I was hoping that she was right.

A few days later, the Newmans offered to finance my college education for me. Mrs. Newman knew from the description of my hospital work in Ottawa how fascinating and fulfilling I thought a nursing career would be. I was so surprised by the offer that I did not know what to say. Finally, I decided that I could not accept it, not knowing whether I could ever repay them. I did, however, accept everything else they offered. Mrs. Newman knew of my passion for music and would occasionally stick a concert ticket under my door. Another time she told me of a community choir that was accepting new members. She also encouraged me to begin writing poetry again. Because of her encouragement, music and poetry once again became part of my life.

On rainy days, when I was not working, I would sit by my small bedroom window and let my imagination wander. That was my favorite time to write. Often my memories took me back home to when I would sit by my third-floor window to write poetry and lyrics to classical music.

Once Mr. Newman could see that I was not going to change my mind about his offer to pay for college, he suggested I at least get my high school diploma. After some hesitation, I tested at a local high school in Chicago and passed. It was gratifying to hold that certificate in my hand. At Mrs. Newman's bidding, I took advanced adult education algebra and chemistry classes and surprised myself with my progress. After all, math had been my least favorite subject back home. Seeing how well I did in those two courses, Mrs. Newman said, "Just in case you change your mind about going into nursing, you know that we will support you."

In early spring the Newmans, with persuasive input from their daughters, began planning their summer vacation. After consulting piles of brochures and discussing each with me, they decided to take a trip to Ireland to visit their daughter. When I asked them where I should go on my first vacation in the United States, they suggested taking a sightseeing bus to one of the national parks—and so I did! Before leaving on my adventure, though, I purchased a small camera to take along; I wanted to bring pictures home to share with the Newmans. In late-Summer we left on our trips the same day—they to Dublin and I to Arizona to see the Grand Canyon.

I boarded the tour bus in downtown Chicago and for the next few days gazed out the window in wonder as I traversed the continent. Everything I saw enthralled me—the sleepy towns, the flat Midwestern plains, and the blue sky against the desert mountains. On day three of our trip, we arrived at the canyon's rim. Nothing had prepared me for its majestic grandeur; at each photo stop there was more to take in. *"Oh, what a beautiful world God had created for us to enjoy."* I thought, *"Is the Lord trying to tell me something?"* I felt as though I was in a holy place outside of time, reaching out for the intangible peace and love that surrounded me and that I so longed for. Late that afternoon, as the sun started to set, we stopped to see the sun paint the rocks in reds and oranges. On the western edge of the canyon, the rocks were soft purple and gray. My camera could capture only the colors but not how I felt inside. Mesmerized, I did not want to leave, but my fellow travelers were boarding the bus. It was time to go home. I promised myself I would return someday.

True to my word, the following year, vacation time could not come soon enough. In late-Summer, I bought a one-way ticket to Denver, Colorado, where I took some driving lessons. After a few days of practice, with license in hand, I bought a small used car. Time did not permit me to go back to the Grand Canyon; instead, I opted for the Royal Gorge in Colorado Springs. Though reluctant, I drove over the suspension bridge that gently swayed in the wind. Relieved to reach the other side, I marveled at the technology and ingenuity that made such a crossway possible.

With each turn in the road, my love and admiration for this country grew and I started to understand the respect and gratitude Americans had for their homeland. Would I feel the same one day? Would I ever be able to become a citizen? I hoped so.

My return to Chicago was also a rewarding experience. Fall was settling over the country and trees started displaying their fiery colors. I stopped many times along the way to take pictures of large fields being harvested by machines, leaving clouds of dust behind them. Along the secondary highways where I traveled, I saw color-ful woodlands and quaint villages with small churches surrounded by equally small graveyards and old abandoned barns.

Whenever possible, whether at a service station or a lunch stop, I started up conversations with whoever was willing to talk. I wanted to know what America was made of besides beautiful land-scapes. At one of my lunch stops I talked to an old gentleman sitting on a bench outside the coffee shop, babysitting his two-month-old great-grand son. "He is my pride and joy; there isn't anything that I wouldn't do for him," he said. His eyes sparkled with joy and love as he gently placed the baby into the stroller. He then proudly showed me a picture of his daughter who worked in the coffee shop as a waitress. Before leaving, I promised to send him a copy of the picture that I had taken of his great-grand son. "What a beautiful family you have," I told him as I left. I could see the pride he took in his family and the joy he had in his life. His face captured what I saw over and over on this trip: love of family and country. I wanted to be part of this energy!

As I approached the outskirts of Chicago, I stopped in one of the suburbs where I saw half a dozen ladies having a yard sale in their church's parking lot. The crowd drew my attention. When I asked about the occasion for the sale, they said they were raising money to purchase musical instruments for their youth and had worked a whole year on the items they were selling. Among the crafts I found some beautiful little baskets and could not resist getting one for Mrs. Newman.

I was looking forward to coming home to share my stories. I knew Mr. Newman, who also loved travel and photography, would especially enjoy my narrated slideshow. Although the pictures documented the places I had been, neither they nor my own words could capture how the mountains, canyons, clear starry nights, and the people had affected me.

Traveling alone had given me time to think about my past, including the cruel treatment that I had experienced in Czechoslovakia for being German and in Bavaria for being an intruder. I asked myself so many questions. Will I be able to erase the horrible memories of the death march to Pohořelice? Can I forgive my former countrymen for a war that killed millions and decimated so many cities, so much land, and so many dreams? Will I be able to bond with the beauty and opportunities of my new home? Will I be accepted in this country? Will I be able to find a church where I can once again hear God's voice? I dared to hope that I would find the answers!

Before the Newmans left Chicago to transfer to India, we had our farewell dinner, at which time I presented them with an album of photographs that I had taken of them at some of their social functions. Warmed by many happy memories, we embraced and said goodbye.

We corresponded for many years. In each of Mrs. Newman's letters, she described in great detail all the wonderful receptions and parties she attended, so well, that I felt as though I had been there with her. Her photos and exotic foreign postage stamps always fed my imagination, making her friendship even more precious. In every letter, she always asked whether I had found a church home, yet. I hoped that one day soon I would be able to write back that I had. In the meantime I was alone with myself and with my questions.

About the same time the Newmans left for India, Johanna, my friend whom I had left in Canada, married a retiring U.S. service man and settled in Charleston, South Carolina. When she heard that once again I was "homeless," she invited me to come and live with her and her husband. I gladly accepted!

Mrs. Gerald A. Newman, wife of the Canadian Consul General. I lived with and worked for the Newmans as a housekeeper for two years while they served in Chicago.

The Grand Canyon is a sacred place for me and is one of the many reasons I fell in love with the United States.[8]

---

8   Paul Fundenburg, available under Creative Commons attribution license.

CHAPTER THIRTEEN

Making a Home in the South

THOUGH I WAS EAGER to see Johanna again and explore the South—an area of the United States that was new to me—I had grown fond of Chicago, my first American home. My relationship with the Newmans had become a true friendship. I was going to miss them as well as the concerts, museums, and plays that had become such a rich part of my life. I would even miss the noise of the city streets that I could hear from my bedroom. The rush of traffic and rattling trains reminded me that I was living in a land of free enterprise and ingenuity where God-given talents knew no boundaries. But I was ready to move on to other parts of this land.

Just before I had left Chicago, I received the news that my Father had passed away. Steffi wrote that he died peacefully in his sleep after suffering from a heart condition. He was laid to rest next to Mother. In my letter to Steffi, I thanked her for having taken care of him and apologized for not having been able to be there with her.

After the Newmans left for India, I secured and closed the residence and turned the keys in to the Canadian Consulate for the new diplomats. Reluctantly, I packed my two-seater and headed south. After a fifteen-hour trip, I arrived at Johanna's doorstep, tired but happy to see her and her husband—but not ready for Charleston's hot and humid weather! Johanna assured me with a smile, "You'll get used to it; I did."

Between tours of old downtown mansions and sprawling plantations, I learned about Charleston's rich history. Well over three centuries had passed since England first set its sights on the fertile oceanfront. Back in 1670, King Charles sent Ashley Cooper, one of England's Lord Proprietors, to develop the land. Soon the city became the center of the British Empire, a corridor for trade and commerce. Sailing vessels from Europe, the West Indies, and Barbados found Charleston Harbor a convenient port on its western edge. At times, over one hundred ships were anchored in Charleston Harbor. Some held goods and others carried settlers who ended up dramatically shaping the economy and character of the region such as the Middletons from Bermuda, the Lowndes and Rawlins from St. Kitts, and the Lucases from Antigua.

Henry Middleton became a wealthy planter and was briefly the president of the Continental Congress. His son Thomas was well known in military affairs, reaching the rank of colonel during the Revolution; his brother Arthur was one of the signers of the Declaration of Independence.

The Lucas family was well known as ship builders in Antigua and settled in Charleston to continue their lucrative business. By 1766, when Lord Montagu came over from England to be the first royal governor to the province of South Carolina, Charleston was on its way to its golden age of trade, law, and schooling.

As I walked the streets of downtown with tour book in hand, I learned that the name of nearly every street tells part of the city's political history. Rutledge Avenue and Pinckney Street are named after two signers of the Constitution. Calhoun Street is named after John C. Calhoun, the inimitable states' rights advocate who served as a senator, congressman, and vice president. Charleston's rich cultural heritage was evident at every turn as well. In the grand two-and three-hundred-year-old mansions I saw the artistry of Charleston's architects of silversmiths, cabinetmakers, and painters. Many religious groups were also drawn to the city. The French Huguenots and Palatines came during the early formation of the province and German Lutherans, among others followed in the 1800s. Soon the city was called "The Holy City" with church steeples ascending on nearly every city block.

Just a few miles outside of downtown were what made this vibrant city life possible: cotton, indigo, and rice plantations. I was impressed by how well preserved some of them were. Walking on their garden paths, I could visualize the landowners strolling in the shade of one-hundred-year-old, moss-draped oak trees. Not within sight of where I walked, their slaves had labored in the fields, fueling a prosperous economy. After the Civil War, when slaves were given their freedom, the landowners could not sustain their plantations. They abandoned these fertile fields and moved to their summer homes in Charleston, where they tried their hand at new ventures in business and industry. Many of the freed slaves continued working for these same families.

After several days of historical sightseeing, Johanna took me to the beach. It was my first close view of the ocean. Walking along the water's edge at Sullivan's Island, with its lighthouse close by, a sense of serenity and freedom surrounded me. The steady rhythm of the ocean pulled me to settle in Charleston as did the city's place in American history. I loved visiting Fort Moultrie, where the colonists defended themselves against the British, and later the Confederates against Union soldiers.

The colonists had defended their freedom and the Confederates a way of life. The country had won the first war and the South had lost the second. I knew what it was like to live where a war had been lost—the despair that rattles around in your heart, the shame that fills the streets.

Though Charleston's history was new to me, I understood it. The city's loss had shaped its history as Germany's had shaped my own. I let myself wonder what the results would have been had Germany won World War II—unimaginable! I could not bear the thought and immediately put it out of my mind, grateful for landing in a country whose future had been secured by the Constitution and the Bill of Rights. I felt at home on the city's narrow, cobblestone streets that reminded me of Germany and knew I would be happy here.

While looking for a job the following couple of days, I kept seeing an ad in the local newspaper for a position at a hotel in downtown Charleston. Although I had no experience in the travel or tourism industry and had never felt drawn to that kind of work, I finally cut out the ad and made an appointment for an interview.

When I met the general manager, Jim Madden, I felt like I was meeting an old friend; he must have felt the same about me. We talked about the different countries we had traveled to and compared our favorite European foods. I talked about my mother's delicious homemade dumplings with roast pork and bib-lettuce salad. His favorite was roast duck, Viennese style. An hour into our conversation we finally discussed my reason for my being there. Even then, he did not discuss the position he wanted filled; but rather asked me whether I was interested in learning the hotel business from the ground up. If I was, he was willing to teach me. I did not know what to expect, but I enthusiastically accepted his offer. That first year I worked in every department of the hotel—washing dishes, tending bar, manning the reception desk, and conducting the night audit.

I appreciated learning from Mr. Madden, who came from a long line of hotel owners. For the next two years, my mentor sent me to all the Hotel Institute programs and seminars the industry had to offer. In addition to learning about managing personnel, I was also trained in budgeting, purchasing, marketing, and planning for banquets and meetings. I loved it all! One New Year's Eve I even forfeited celebrating with friends to help one auditor balance her books that night. It took the two of us until 3:30 a.m. to find the error and balance the books for the month. My reward: a delicious home-cooked dinner, prepared by my colleague the following evening.

After returning from one of the seminars, I received a promotion to assistant manager. Later I learned that having lived in the United States for five years, I was eligible for citizenship. But could I meet all the requirements? I needed to read, write and converse in English as well as demonstrate a basic knowledge of American history and the structure of the U.S. government. By the end of June, I had completed a citizenship class and passed all of the required tests. On July 4, 1964, I took the oath of allegiance to the United States and was sworn in to become a U.S. citizen.

Walking out of that courthouse, I finally felt like a human being! I now lived in a country where no one could expel me or take away my constitutional rights as a citizen. This was a Republic, not a dictatorship or socialist regime where the citizens had no voice in selecting their leadership. Now I could vote for candidates I thought would positively shape the future of my new homeland. What an honor and what a blessing!

However, until I found someone to share my life with, how could I be completely at home? I enjoyed exploring Charleston and found work very satisfying, but at the end of each workday and after every book I read and every excursion I took, I returned to my small apartment—alone.

Two weeks after I became a United States citizen, I met Ray, a local policeman who had come to the hotel to complete an investigation. We were immediately attracted to each other. I had not dated since I left Chicago and was eager to get to know this attractive, six-foot tall, blond-haired and blue-eyed Charleston native with a bright, contagious smile. At the conclusion of his business, he asked me to have dinner with him and I accepted.

After two weeks of dating, Ray proposed. Marriage had certainly not been in my plans, but I was swept off of my feet and accepted!

The announcement came as a surprise to all our friends. Those who knew us well made wagers about how long our marriage would last. We laughed at the results: his friends gave him only six months because of his previous marriage, and my friends thought we would last only twice that; they did not think that I was ready to settle down. Had we been the betting kind, all of them would have lost. Ray and I were married for over twenty-five years.

The first few involved a lot of learning and adjusting—which at times were difficult for both of us. My husband was a forty-four-year-old Charlestonian who had a nineteen-year-old son from a previous marriage. I was a foreigner, eight years his junior, who needed to learn to cook Southern food. It was not easy, but with time we learned to adjust.

Among other things, we had discussed religion and church attendance before we married. Raymond, Jr., a College of Charleston student, attended a downtown Baptist church on Sundays, with his girlfriend. His father, though a member, said that he did not go to church because he had difficulties applying the church's teachings to his work as a police officer. Despite our many discussions, I did not understand his decision. I even suggested that he see the pastor of his church for counseling and guidance, but he ignored me.

His silence troubled me, so whenever he worked the evening shift and I was home alone with my thoughts, I turned on his police scanner to get a better picture in my mind of what he faced in his line of work. After about two weeks of listening to all that went on in the city streets, I came to the conclusion that Ray worked in a dangerous and cruel world. I started to understand why he did not want to talk about his day. He had lived in this other world for so many years that he had probably forgotten the meaning of loving kindness and human understanding. No wonder he was often irritable, short in his responses, and absent-minded. Perhaps his behavior was a result of his inability to express his inner feelings. My hopes to share and discuss spiritual questions with him went unfulfilled. I thought of Uncle Hugo. Oh, how I longed for his advice. Now that I was an adult, a heart-to-heart conversation with him would have been so meaningful and comforting. Discouraged and with no confidante with whom I could share my thoughts, I decided not to attend Ray's church or any other. Over the years, I never mentioned the subject of religion again. I too turned silent.

Once Raymond, Jr. had graduated from the College of Charleston and left home to attend the University of South Carolina in Columbia, Ray and I decided to move to the country and build a small home in Berkeley County on Lake Moultrie, about forty miles north of Charleston. It was both satisfying and challenging to clear the land ourselves, help the contractor with construction detail, and together figure out what we wanted in our retirement home.

After several months, the day of moving in arrived. After settling in, we realized that all the problems and headaches with the contractor had been worth it. It was a beautiful, cozy home with a big front porch and large picture windows that wrapped around the living room and the L-shaped dining room. At the end of that first day in our new home, I sat on the porch in a big rocking chair, overlooking the trees with the lake in the distance and I realized how far I had come and how blessed I was to have a place of my own; I was sure Ray felt the same.

Given how irritable Ray had been when he came home from work, I thought that retiring from the police force would make him happier—less prickly. But I could tell he was not satisfied and when I asked, he avoided my questions. Over time, his frustration turned to verbal abuse; at other times he would not speak at all. As soon as I came home from work, he would either barely speak to me or get into a rage over insignificant things. On my days off, to avoid talking to me, he would find some place to go or work in the garage. He would not tell me what was bothering him.

I managed to control my emotions at home and at work, but during the one-hour drive back and forth, I cried and wondered what I should do. If I chose to leave him, where would I go? I had no one to turn to.

Or did I?

One morning, on my way to work and desperate for answers, I started talking to God. I told Him that over the years I had forgotten how to pray. "If you're still there," I continued, "please listen to me and answer me in a way I will understand." Soon a soothing warmth surrounded me and a sense of indescribable comfort, love and relief came over me. I knew it was God's presence and that He had not forsaken or forgotten me here in Charleston, nor in Mrs. Nováková's tiny shed nor even in the unfriendly church in Germany. Tears welled up as I thanked Him for coming back into my life. Then, in complete trust and faithful acceptance, I opened my heart to Him, just as I had as a child. As I drove home that evening, I spoke aloud of my most pressing concerns: that I was angry with my husband and wanted his attitude toward me to change. That same day I had an unforgettable experience: God responded to my prayer. At first the most wonderful, comforting feeling came over me and my heart filled with a new sense of happiness and calm. Then I received an impression that was clear but surprising to me. I needed to change my attitude towards Ray! Although I was taken aback, I instantly accepted the message and my desperation disappeared almost immediately. The most liberating feeling came over me. Coming home that night, instead of not talking, I returned to making normal conversation with Ray, asking him what he wanted to drink with his dinner. "Iced tea will be fine," he answered. I had prepared dried lima beans and ham the day before, which was Ray's favorite dish, and after coming home from work I cooked some rice and green vegetables. During dinner I asked him what was new, and he told me what had happened in the neighborhood while I was at work that day. He and the neighbor had gone fishing and brought home a bucketful of fish. "I'll clean them and get them ready for the freezer if you want me to," Ray said. I answered, "That would be wonderful, thanks. We can cook some on the weekend." The realization and acceptance of a wonderful lesson from the Lord marked a new beginning in our relationship.

The next morning I thanked the Lord for His love and for not giving up on me. I asked how I could feel closer to Him. I cried as I told Him how long I had missed that close relationship I had enjoyed as a child in Uncle Hugo's church where I could feel His presence. I missed Him and the conversations Uncle Hugo and I had about Him; most of all, I missed my heartfelt prayers, when I had felt His presence only a touch away and could hear Him whisper, "Go in peace, my child."

And once again He guided me. He told me, that as an adult, I needed to attend a church where I would learn all that I needed to know about Him, His doctrine, and His kingdom. That evening, on my way home, I told the Lord that I was working most Sundays and could not attend church. By then I was comfortable talking to my newfound friend, confident that I would again receive an answer.

The following morning when I arrived at the office, the general manager, Mr. Clark, who had been substituting for Mr. Madden while my boss was in the hospital, asked to see me. Though I could tell from his reddened face and stern voice that he was outraged, I had no idea why—so what followed came as a complete surprise. When I entered his office, he said sharply, "Margit, I have no other choice but to let you go. You are fired." Stunned, I asked what prompted his extreme reaction. Then suddenly, before he could say anything,

I remembered balancing the petty cash in the safe the night before and finding a discrepancy of five hundred dollars. I surmised that he did not want to be accountable to me for his dishonest transaction and decided to let me go. "No reason," he abruptly answered. "As a matter of fact," he said, "the home office said that your work is exemplary and every report is timely and accurate. But I have to let you go nonetheless." His response confirmed my suspicion. With me gone, he could cover his tracks.

At first, I was devastated, having worked my way up for so many years only to receive this as a reward. As I sat down at my desk, my evening prayer came to my mind. Then, I realized that this turn of events had been the answer to my prayers. I was now able to go to church on Sundays. Suddenly, I felt relief wash over me to replace my bitterness. I had never thought that getting fired from a job would make me happy, especially one that I was good at and enjoyed so much! That day, I learned that the Lord moves in mysterious ways.

On my way home that night, unemployed for the first time since I began working at age eighteen, I realized that Easter was only three days away and I could attend services. Oh, how I looked forward to going to church—though I did not yet know which one. Over the years I had been searching for the Lord's church, one that taught constant and true principles, one where I would feel at home. What a glorious Easter celebration it would be if I could find such a church. Before reaching home that night, I put my request into my prayer, knowing that I would get an answer before Sunday.

All day Saturday I was busy doing household chores and preparing Easter dinner when one of my neighbors came by to visit. Though we were friends, Jerri was not aware of my recent spiritual experiences or my past marital difficulties. Just before leaving, she stopped at the door and asked, "Would you like to go to church with me on Sunday?"

Surprised, I uttered, "I would love to. Thank you," knowing that God's spirit had spoken through her and that I had acknowledged in kind. I had been invited to and had attended a few social functions at Jerri's church, The Church of Jesus Christ of Latter-day Saints, but had not been interested in learning anything about it. This invitation was different.

I felt as though someone had poured a bucket of water over me; it was electrifying.

The next day was a most bright and beautiful Easter Sunday. When I entered the door to the church and walked into the vestibule, one of the church leaders, Brother Vasquez, came down the long hallway to welcome me. He had a bright smile as he shook my hand and his words sounded so sincere, as if he had met me before and was welcoming me back. I stood there, unable to speak at first. My mind took me back to Uncle Hugo's church. Although this modern building was only a few years old and nothing like the tiny sanctuary where he and I had worshipped, I felt comfortable, almost as if I had been there before. As I stood there, the presence of God felt so real that a sense of serenity came over me. I was finally in God's house, where I could feel His spirit and where He wanted me to be. I hoped that at last I would receive an answer to the question that had chased me for thirty years: *Is the torture of innocent people forgivable by God?* As always, other questions followed, but this time somehow I knew one day the answers would come. In that vestibule I felt like a world traveler, who after a long journey, puts her baggage down, and says with a sigh, *"It's so good to be home!"*

I said to myself, *"Thank you, Uncle Hugo, for bringing me home!"*

My husband Raymond in 1964, age forty

Johanna and me after a day of exploring
beautiful Charleston, South Carolina

CHAPTER FOURTEEN

Finding God's House

As I ENTERED the small chapel, it looked as I had imagined it would—plain but inviting, with about ten rows of chairs, five on each side of the center aisle. A hymn book lay on every other chair. I wondered what kind of hymns they contained and whether I would be able to learn all of them. From the prelude music that someone was playing on a small organ in the far corner of the chapel, I could tell that I probably would. Some of the melodies were familiar to me. On each side of the speaker's stand was a large arrangement of Easter lilies, the only decorations in the room. The simplicity made me feel comfortable and at home.

After Jerri and I took our seats, a gentleman came to the pulpit and made several announcements. Then the organist played the introduction to the opening hymn, *"Christ the Lord is Risen Today."* The chapel was filled to capacity and the congregation's strong voices were energizing. I knew the melody and sang the beautiful, uplifting lyrics. Then a young man in the seat in front of me gave an opening prayer. He thanked the Lord for the opportunity to celebrate Easter, for Christ's atoning sacrifice and His resurrection on our behalf. I could tell that the young man was moved by his own prayer, and I was touched by the sincerity in his voice. He then asked for God's blessings on the church family and those less fortunate.

I had to think back on other church services I had attended—the Catholics who offered prayers from their Book of Prayers and other churches where the pastor offered one. For me, a prayer from a member of the congregation had so much more meaning and helped me feel more connected to God's Spirit and to the congregation. After the passing of the sacrament, we watched a special video with an intermittent narrative about the life of Christ and His crucifixion. The presentation was very moving and I felt humbled but grateful, as I thought of the pain and agony He had borne for us. The program concluded with His resurrection. As I looked around the congregation, their wet cheeks told me that they were as moved as I was. The choir then concluded the meeting with a special rendition of the Hallelujah chorus from Handel's *"Messiah."* Their beautiful voices reminded me of some of the choirs that I had belonged to in the past. I hoped that I could join this choir someday. The closing prayer concluded a very special Easter Sunday service for me, one that I knew I would remember for many years to come. I felt very humbled and edified. This was the church that God had led me to; I could feel His Spirit surrounding me, and I knew I had come home. Before leaving the building, Jerri introduced me to some of the members of the congregation, all of whom welcomed me and asked me to come back. I knew I would.

The next day marked the beginning of two new experiences: an earnest study of the Gospel and unemployment. I spent a beautiful spring at home with time to read and study every day. Jerri kept me supplied with plenty of study material. There was so much to learn. Once a week she and her husband Murl invited me to their house to enjoy an evening of scripture study with their family. One evening, Murl talked about the restoration of Christ's church here on earth and read from the Book of Mormon, an ancient scripture discovered in the 1820s. I listened to the presentation but did not ask many questions. Even though everything he taught me was new to me, it all made sense. On my way home, before going into the house, I sat on the front porch for a while, thinking of all the things I had learned, when a deep sense of conviction came over me. The spirit testified to me that the church I was learning about was the only one with *all* the truth. I still had many questions but was certain that in time I would receive answers to them as well.

That spring was full of discovery and learning with Jerri's family, at church and in my own living room, but I was on this journey alone. Ray chose to do other things whenever I invited him to church or went to Jerri's home. When I asked for his input or shared what I was learning, he did not comment. Although he did not share my newly found faith and seemed disinterested, for my birthday that year he surprised me with a trip to the open house at the Atlanta, Georgia Temple. I was so surprised and happy when he offered to take me. As we walked through the magnificent building I had the feeling that Ray too was touched by the spirit but just could not or would not express his feelings.

Three months after that memorable Easter service and my visit to the open house in Atlanta, I was baptized on July 19, 1981; another turning point in my life. I thought of all the bends and crossroads in my life, that the Lord had led me through: the Silos at the Experimental Station in Pohořelice where I hid from Russian soldiers who were looking for women to abduct; the Romanian soldiers' soup kitchen who supplied life-saving meals for Mother and me; the barrel in which I hid in our apartment after returning from the country so the Russian soldiers could not find me; the interview before Czech government officials where my outspoken manner could have caused me to be arrested. All along He protected me and sent angels to guide me out of whatever dangerous situation I was in: Mrs. Novaková, who helped me survive 1945; the Russian Lady Officer who fed me and Mother and gave me the Army boots; Steffi, who lovingly helped me over many emotional hurdles, just as Mother would have done. During all my trials, I was never without protection. The hand of the Lord had always been upon me and I was grateful.

Anchored in my faith, I felt ready to return to work. I found a job with the County Clerk of Court's office, where I learned the rules and procedures of the legal system in this country. There was so much for me to learn between the filing of the first document and the final verdict in court. As I learned to navigate the intricacies of the legal system, I was impressed with the different laws that protect the innocent and aim to provide justice. I was impressed in one particular instance, a murder case, in which the safeguarding of all evidence had been crucial in ultimately finding the accused not guilty.

After the first six months, I was deputized and had the privilege of working with the chief deputy, Mildred Hood, a native of Berkeley County, who was very active in the state's Genealogical and Historical Society. She handled the dockets for every presiding judge in all of the civil and criminal terms of court in the county. Mildred and I soon became good friends. She invited me to attend several plantation tours that the Berkeley County Historical Society sponsored. While exploring the grounds I learned about the Society's preservation projects, one of which involved locating and recording all the cemeteries and graves in the county for historical preservation as well as genealogical purposes. I knew there were many churches and cemeteries in the county dating back to colonial times. The thought of being in their presence and being part of documenting their history for posterity gave me a feeling of continuity that I had never felt in my own country. Being a new member of a church that taught me the importance of conducting genealogical research and connecting to my ancestors drew me to this project. When I learned of the details and I saw the enthusiasm in Mildred's face, I said, "Let's get started tomorrow!"

Though Berkeley County has fewer tourists and gets less press, it, in many ways has as rich a history as Charleston. St. John's Berkeley Parish was created by the South Carolina Assembly Act of 1704. The first church was called Biggin Hill (later only Biggin). Built in its present location around 1711 and burned in a forest fire in 1755, it was rebuilt in 1761. During the Revolution, British troops used Biggin Church as a depot; in 1781, as they retreated from the colonists' attacks, the church and the stores around it were burned.

Again, it was rebuilt, only to be damaged during the Civil War and later burned again by a forest fire; the remaining structure fell into disrepair. Today, only two walls and the cemetery remain, reminding visitors of a rich history.

Another jewel of historical significance is Strawberry Chapel in the lower part of St. John's, Berkeley. It was built as a parochial chapel of ease in 1725 and served the town of Childsbury, which today no longer exists. The beautiful chapel still stands and holds some of the artifacts saved after the fires at Biggin Church. The surrounding cemetery with its decorative markers reminds us of some of the parishioners' wealth during colonial times.

When the final call came for volunteers for this preservation project, Mildred and I had already mapped out the area and took on the task with fervor; we worked on weekends, holidays, and even lunch breaks. We drove out into the country to locate long-forgotten cemeteries and placed their locations on a county grid map, inventoried the stones, and indexed all individuals' names. Where there was only partial information, we recorded whatever and however it appeared on the marker. We then indexed all map locations, cemetery names, and individual names.

We had no trouble receiving permission from caretakers and landowners to enter private property. The only adversaries we occasionally encountered, mainly during the warm summer months, were swarms of bees, yellow jackets, and an occasional snake—none of which deterred us for long.

By the completion of the project two years later in 1985, I had come to know and love every bend in those back roads. When the Berkeley County Library was remodeled and a time capsule was placed in the corner stone of the new wing, our four-hundred-page cemetery book, with nearly ten thousand inscriptions, was among the items chosen to be preserved there. Before the book was published, Mildred and I took flyers about our project to the National Genealogical Society's annual convention in Salt Lake City, Utah, and sent one to every library, historical, and genealogical group in our state. The demand for our book was so great that it sold out before it was even published!

Besides the satisfaction of helping preserve historical information, compiling this inventory had another effect on me. While walking among the tombstones in the peace and solitude of the burial grounds, I often thought of the individuals whose names I was recording and wondered what kind of lives they had led and how they had died. At times we found thought-provoking inscriptions. I came across such a stone at Strawberry Chapel. It was made of white marble and shaped like a cradle. Hanging by chains from two posts, the stone read, "We loved you so." On the other side, I was unable to make out the name; only the date was legible: 1824. I wondered how the baby had died and whether the parents had other children. Another memorable marker I found was that of a slave. On one of the plantations, along a path going through the woods toward the main house, I found the tablet that read "Ben, a faithful servant. Rest in Peace 1850." I thought of the bond the master must have had to his slave to recognize him in this way.

Another gravestone I recall was that of a Confederate soldier who fell ill on his way home from the battlefields. He was taken in by a kindhearted farmer who nursed him and later gave him his final resting place under a big oak tree. The writing on the tablet was faded but legible: "He served God and his country well, 1864." I thought of the soldier's loved ones who waited in vain for his return from the war.

We were grateful to the landowners who let us preserve some of the history in their county. Upon completion of our project, we returned to the three memorable gravesites and placed some flowers as a gesture of gratitude and as a tribute to the liberties we enjoy in this land.

Many times during this project, my thoughts wandered to my parents, who were buried in a foreign, unfriendly land. I wished that I could put some flowers on their last resting place— just once. I also thought of my grandparents' graves in Brno, my birthplace. When I was a child, every year on All Saints' Day, Mother and I placed flowers and candles on her parents' graves. I wondered whether their grave markers had been preserved or been used for more "useful purposes" by the cold and heartless Communist regime.

Mildred was also interested in genealogy and family history. In her living room, she had a large piece of tapestry hanging with multiple generations and several binders filled with information on her family. Although her reason for doing genealogy was different from mine, with her help I started compiling my own family tree. She suggested first finding my siblings and then gathering all the documents about my family I could get. I knew it would not be an easy task, but I was determined to learn all I could. After Erwin had left the farm in Bavaria, he moved wherever job opportunities presented themselves; after he married, he and his family moved several times to wherever reconstructed apartment buildings went up, each time seeking improved housing conditions. Lilli lived in the suburbs of Heilbronn for several years and then, after she married, moved only once. When her husband's job called for a transfer to Frankfurt, she lost contact with our mobile brother and had no way of informing him of her whereabouts. By the time I had moved from Canada to the United States, I had lost contact with both of them. Compiling a family tree, therefore, would not be an easy task. Occasionally, I would launch a search by correspondence to their last known address with the request to "Please forward," but all the letters came back with the caption "Cannot forward." I realized I needed help and called my friend Johanna, whose brother was an official at police headquarters in Munich, Germany, and asked her to contact him to see whether he could help me in my search. I gave her all personal statistics and the last known addresses I had for both. He agreed to help.

Soon he discovered that Lilli was living in Frankfurt, Germany, and Erwin was about an hour farther north on the Rhein river, in the small town of Bingen. He had found not only their addresses but also their phone numbers. I was so happy to find both of them. Talking to one another on the phone for the first time in over thirty-five years was overwhelming. Between the tears of joy rolling down my face and Lilli's crying, we sisters could not say very much. We promised to write and send pictures.

When I called Erwin, he was so surprised he couldn't speak and handed the phone over to his wife Lina, while he collected himself. I had never met her or heard her voice, but in our brief exchange I felt as though I was reconnecting with an old friend. We promised to send pictures and vowed never to lose touch again. Correspondence began almost immediately among the three of us with phone calls crossing the Atlantic on holidays and birthdays. It felt wonderful to get reacquainted!

In one of my letters I told them that I was compiling our family tree and asked them to send me copies of whatever documents, pictures and mementos they had and were willing to share. Soon the thick, brown envelopes started arriving with letters and pictures, some of which I had seen as a child but had long forgotten. Erwin sent me a copy of his wedding picture and photos of his two children. Lilli did the same. Although I treasured these precious keepsakes, they did not include the genealogical information about my parents and grandparents that I was looking for. I wanted to know all I could: where I came from and who my ancestors were.

Since direct contact with the archives or parishes in Czechoslovakia was not possible, I wrote to the Czech Embassy in Washington, D.C. to ask for their help in obtaining my grandparents' marriage certificate. It would give me the names of the bride's and groom's parents and where they came from—all information that could lead me to another generation. I gave them all the facts they needed: my grandparents' names, birthdates, and birthplaces, as well as the parish church where they were married. After several months of waiting, I received notice that because this genealogy was what they called a "non-productive" activity, they would have to hire a special researcher to find what I was looking for. Though the fee seemed high, I paid for the service—hopeful that I would receive a copy of the original marriage certificate.

About six months passed before I heard back. Instead of receiving a copy of the original, I got an excerpt from the original with only information I already had. Old, bitter feelings surfaced along with utter disappointment over the results of my inquiry. I was dealing with a Communist regime that had forced me to endure its prejudice and hatred after the war. "Oh God," I pleaded, "Will I ever be able to forget the past? Please help me heal and teach me to forgive." With this prayer in my heart, I decided that I would have to be satisfied with the information I had on my ancestors. Many branches and limbs on my family tree would remain blank.

That same year, 1989, after nearly three decades since its construction, the Berlin Wall came down. I hoped that perhaps the wall in my heart could as well. Within an hour of the announcement, my brother and sister called to celebrate the good news that the borders between East and West had reopened. Erwin said, "We should be able to drive into Czechoslovakia now." Lilli suggested that we three have a family reunion to celebrate. Erwin agreed. I promised to come to Germany in 1991.

Soon Lilli called to tell me, "I have heard from our cousin Hedwick. You remember her, don't you? She still lives in Czechoslovakia and wants us to come and visit." How she had found her was still a mystery at this point, but with the Iron Curtain down, such breakthroughs were not as hard to come by. A few months later, ready with notepaper, my childhood diaries, a camera, and a half-empty briefcase to hold documents I hoped to find, I started on my trip to Europe. Too anxious to sleep on my overnight flight from Atlanta to Frankfurt, I had lots of time to think and reflect on the last time I crossed the Atlantic by boat from Bremerhafen to Halifax, Nova Scotia, and the family I had left behind in Europe. I was eagerly anticipating seeing all the changes that had taken place in Germany, as well as reuniting with my brother and sister and meeting their children.

When I arrived at the Frankfurt Airport the following morning, over twenty people were there to greet me. Some I had not met yet, but as soon I was introduced as "Tante Margit," (Aunt Margit), I knew that I was meeting nephews and nieces. Lilli and Erwin each had a boy and a girl.

Since Erich, my brother's son, lived just around the corner from his father and had the bigger house, I spent the night with him and his family. After a long morning visit with all of them, Erwin, Lilli and I loaded Erwin's station wagon and headed for Lilli's summer vacation home in the Black Forest, where the three of us would celebrate our reunion. As we drove through the countryside of Würtemberg and farther into Bavaria, Erwin suggested taking a short side trip to the small country church and cemetery where our parents and Steffi were buried. Lilli and I agreed. As we purchased some flowers in the town nearby, Lilli told us that over the years she had corresponded with the parish office there and had found that Father's and Steffi's graves were close to Mother's. At the time of Father's death, Steffi was able to obtain a gravesite close to my mother's for him. When she passed away, the farmer couple she had lived with provided a site for her on their family plot. They had taken care of her grave all the years in gratitude for her services.

With Lilli's help, I fulfilled a wish I had during the cemetery project in Berkeley County—to "just once" clean up and place flowers on my parents' graves. My wish had been granted, and I was very grateful. Before coming to the cemetery, Lilli purchased deep purple and yellow pansies and light blue forget-me-nots. After we cleaned the dead leaves and weeds from the graves, together we planted the flowers. Afterwards, we stood there, silently, each occupied with our own thoughts and prayers. I felt tears rolling down my face, knowing that I would never see the graves again after coming such a distance, but I was grateful for this one-time opportunity.

After two hours on the super-highway, we arrived at Lilli's home nestled in the hills of the Black Forest. Sitting on a slope and surrounded by flowerbeds, her home overlooked an expansive valley and the village of Villingen. After unpacking and relaxing in the comfortable, large living room, Lilli brought out several boxes of mementos and picture albums. We shared long-forgotten childhood memories. I recalled Lilli and Erwin's efforts to teach me to swim in the river close to our apartment building. When I stumbled over a big boulder and fell into the rushing water, they both jumped in to save me from drowning. I never learned how to swim after that!

As our conversation and recollections turned towards the war, Erwin recounted his capture by the British in Italy, and Lilli followed with memories of her own experiences during the last days of war in Germany. When Erwin asked whether I still had my diary, I pulled out a couple of old notebooks from my bag. He used to tease me about them, asking what childish secrets they might contain. Now, he was learning the truth, as I read a few passages about the Christmases without them and how Mother read and reread their most recent letters as we sat in candlelit bomb shelters. By the evening's end, Lilli suggested that I write a family history; she thought there was too much material for us to go through in one evening and she wanted her children to know our history. Erwin agreed. I too was interested in recording our history but hesitated to commit. I was no longer fluent in German or Czech and feared my English was not adequate. I knew three languages but was a master of none. I told them I would think about it.

Lilli then surprised us with a box of pictures and a bundle of letters tied together with a blue ribbon. Mother had written them, when my parents and I were working on the farm and Lilli lived in Heilbronn. Lonely and despairing, Mother had poured her heart out to her oldest child in these letters. In her last one, she expressed her wish not to be buried in Germany, away from her homeland. Lilli told us that she cried bitterly when she read that, feeling the anguish she must have carried, as she wrote this.

I saw tears in Lilli's eyes and I knew how she must have felt then, reading Mother's words. Seeing Mother every day, I too sensed her pain. Though helpless and powerless, we all had no choice but to go on.

We all cried.

I felt prompted to tell my siblings about my religious conversion and the joy I felt about my connection to God. I assured them that He knew of Mother's agony and the things she had to go through. "She is at peace now," I said. "There is no need for us to cry. Her trials are over." I then told them that Christ had died for all of us and through His atoning sacrifice and our repentance we could all be together again, one day. Erwin made no comment, and Lilli said, "You always had a lot of faith as a child. I am glad you have found a church to belong to."

I also told them of Mother's and my experience at Pohořelice—the torture and killing of innocent people we had witnessed on the open road between Brno and Vienna. I shared my desire to find an answer to the question that still lay heavily on my heart: "Are the atrocities of war forgivable by God?" I also wondered aloud, "After all these years, will I finally find peace in Pohořelice?" As I shared my thoughts, I saw in my mind's eye the field in southern Moravia where hundreds of innocent people lay buried without a marker. I was sure that I would find my answers on that stretch of Highway No 461 between Brno and Vienna.

Erwin understood my sense of urgency and suggested that we drive to Czechoslovakia, visit our home town of Brno for a couple of days, and on the way back take the southern route through Austria, which would take us through Pohořelice. Lilli agreed. She called our cousin Hedwick and asked her whether we could come on such short notice. "Of course," Hedwick answered, "I am looking forward to seeing all of you after all these years." My brother, sister and I started making preparations to close down the house and start on our journey the following morning.

I never thought that I would ever see my home town again and now, after forty-five years, it was going to happen. *"If I only could take Mother with me,"* I thought.

In my heart, I did.

Healing My Heart

EARLY THE NEXT MORNING, we packed the car for our journey east. Lilli had spoken with Hedwick at length the night before and had learned about Czechoslovakia's limited access to affordable Western goods, as well as our cousin's impoverished living conditions across the past four and a half decades. Although life slightly improved after the Iron Curtain came down, merchandise in the stores was still beyond their means or not available. Lilli asked Hedwick what she and her family wanted or needed. "What I really need is some good soap powder. The kind we're getting here doesn't get the clothes clean," our cousin replied. Lilli noticed the hesitation in Hedwick's voice. Our cousin needed so much but did not want to ask for more. Finally she said, "My electric sweeper broke down a few days ago and a new one is very expensive. If you happen to have an old used one that still works, I would appreciate receiving it." Lilli cried as she heard Hedwick's humble request. "Do you know of anything your grandchildren would want?" Lilli asked. "Of course," Hedwick replied, "You know how children are. They have been admiring Western clothes ever since the Iron Curtain was lifted. Their list would be endless." Lilli asked for their sizes and promised to bring some of the things they wanted. "I have children of my own," she said. "I understand." She also reassured Hedwick that we were aware of her circumstances and not to worry about accommodating us; we would be happy just to see her and Dagmar's family.

Hedwick had come from a relatively wealthy family before the war. I remember her as a teenager never going without anything she wanted. She was an only child and was raised by her grandmother after her mother died due to complications of her birth. Her father had been director of the library system of our city, a rather prominent and influential position in those days for Brno, a city of nearly three hundred and fifty thousand inhabitants. During the last year of war, Hedwick married a civil engineer, the son of a notable Czech family from Prague. The couple was happy that her father had been able to see her give birth to a baby girl, before he died during the last days of conflict in 1945.

After the war ended, instead of kicking her out for being German, the new revolutionary Czech government confiscated her estate. Her Czech husband, realizing that her father's connections and influence had vanished, divorced her. The government gave her a small three-room farmhouse in the country, where she raised her little girl, Dagmar. The house had no running water or central heat. She carried water from a well in the backyard and used a fireplace to keep warm in winter. She had a single gas burner on which to heat water for baths and laundry as well as cook meals. After forty-five years, she still lived there.

When her wages as a daytime cleaning woman at a local hospital were not enough to put food on the table, she planted a vegetable garden as well as fruit trees and raised honeybees in her backyard for additional income. On weekends, she worked to earn enough money to buy firewood for her fireplace. Although she had received a bachelor's degree from the Brno Teacher's College, she could not get a well-paying job. As with my father, her German ethnicity closed many doors. Determined to give her child a good foundation for life, Hedwick did not let ethnic prejudice dampen her spirit.

As we packed the car for our trip to see our cousin, Lilli suggested we take a side trip to a shopping center to purchase items for Hedwick's family. I remembered the time my family and I lived on the farm in Bavaria and the many things we needed but had to do without, like decent cooking pots and pans and dishes. At mealtimes, we used our cots as chairs and cardboard boxes as tables.

Appliances like a washing machine or a refrigerator were things we only dreamed of. I thought of Hedwick being in a similar situation for over four decades and desperately wanted to help.

As we entered the huge department store, I gazed at the wide selection of merchandise and felt like a Christmas elf ready to gather and deliver gifts for someone who had gone without for too, too long. I headed for the clothing section to buy jeans and shirts for the children as well as fur-lined boots for Hedwick to wear during the winter months when she had to shovel snow to get to the well on her property. Lilli found a vacuum cleaner, a food grinder, some quality kitchen utensils, and a set of stainless steel kitchen knives that would not wear out in a year or two. We also picked out cosmetic items for Hedwick and Dagmar—facial soap, body lotion, shampoo, conditioner, and a manicure set for each of them. We wondered whether we could fit all of our presents in Erwin's car. Somehow he managed to find space for everything.

Once we were on the road again headed for the Black Forest, I remembered the last time that I had seen those tall slender evergreen trees with their long branches swaying in the breeze. The gentle winds flowing through the woods, over the hills and valleys reminded me of an orchestra of string instruments with their gentle chords filling the mind with soothing sounds.

After we left the winding roads of the forest and started driving alongside harvested fields, memories surfaced of harvesting fields in lower Bavaria. When the farmer's family and I finished gathering a crop, I always felt so grateful and secure. The barns, full of hay to feed the animals during the long winter months and of wheat and grains to sustain us, assured me that God provided for all of us— man as well as beast.

Now I gazed at the picturesque villages with domed churches topped with steeples. The shingled rooftops of the farmers' homes as well as the flowerpots that hung from their windows and balconies spoke of their pride and prosperity. In one of the villages, we passed a herd of cows coming home from the pasture with their leather straps and cowbells around their necks; their herders, two tanned, rosy-cheeked boys smiled and waved at us. The country was prospering once again.

A few hours later, as we approached the Czech border, a strange feeling came over me. I remembered the last time that I, along with thousands of others, had crossed this border. Packed into closed cattle cars like animals, we traveled by freight train against our will. We were unwanted, homeless human beings, stripped of all civil and human rights—worthless in the eyes of the Czech government. Our papers read: "Permanently expelled from the Czech Republic."

Although I now held an American passport in my hand, for a moment I felt apprehensive approaching the border patrol. When it was our turn to cross, Erwin, who carried no traumatic memories of Czech authorities cutting him off from his parents, calmly handed the officer our papers. Like Erwin, Lilli too looked un-phased. I was the only living family member who remained nervous. The guard looked in the direction of our car and then again at the passports. Finally, after what felt like hours to me, he stamped them and returned them to my brother. Did only I heave a sigh of relief? Apparently my fear of Czech authority had not dissipated across four and a half decades; for in those moments of waiting, the traumatic expulsion from my homeland felt as though it had just occurred.

I remembered the nightmares I endured during the first few years after we left Brno, each night waking up covered in sweat and facing each new day of hard work exhausted. I had chosen not to tell Mother. Any more stress on her could have been fatal, and Father was away the whole week. When he came home on weekends he was exhausted and preoccupied with safeguarding Mother's health.

With no one to talk to and no medical care available, I was left to live with my own fears.

As Erwin handed me my passport, I instinctively grabbed it with both hands, only to shake my head for overreacting, hoping that my siblings hadn't noticed. After crossing the border and driving into the Bohemian countryside, my anxiety gradually subsided and I could take in the barren fields. The barns that we passed were empty as were the fields. We did not spot even one farmer. I remembered the late summer road trips that I took while I lived in Chicago. I had so enjoyed watching the farmers harvest their fertile fields to supply the country with their abundance of crops. My childhood memories of the Bohemian countryside were the same, but now the fields, idle and neglected, were full of weeds as if they had no life left in them—as if they had been harvested to death and abandoned.

Erwin somehow avoided the road's many potholes while Lilli and I looked in disbelief upon the dreary landscape. As we drove through the villages and small towns, the same picture appeared: streets and homes in dire need of repair. Rusted out road signs, broken down fences, and dirty buildings met us everywhere. The country and its people had been choked by a Communist dictatorship that had stopped free enterprise and productivity for over four decades.

Just as the Berlin Wall had been taken down piece by piece two years before, the wall of anger around my heart started to crumble. In its place came sorrow. Looking around me, I could see that my former countrymen had paid their debt to me. My forced exodus had brought me freedom and happiness. Their freedom from Nazi occupation had brought them Communist oppression and deprivation.

I thought of my last interview with the Czech government official prior to leaving the country, and I wondered what would have become of me had I accepted his offer to stay in the country and "enjoy" the Czech government's free education and room and board. I still remember the short middle-aged man behind his large desk asking me, "Do you wish to continue your education?" Then, with a gesture of grandeur and generosity he said, "My government has an offer to make to you. We are going to educate you, free of charge and give you free room and board." He never indicated what the "free of charge" entailed. Today, imagining it stole my breath.

Erwin woke me from my memories when he pulled into a restaurant along the highway and announced, "Ladies, it's time for lunch." As we exchanged greetings with the owner, I noticed the waitress's efforts to be polite and accommodating. Was this the first sign of free enterprise?

Lilli still spoke enough Czech to make out the menu. When the waitress heard us speaking German, she helped us complete our food order in German as well. My roast pork and dumplings with bib lettuce was excellent and the portion was big enough for two. When Lilli complimented the waitress on the quality of food, the waitress explained, "Since the Berlin Wall came down, the economic restrictions and conditions have relaxed, and we are once again raising our own livestock and growing our own produce."

Lilli asked her where she had learned to speak German so fluently. Smiling, the woman explained, "In Eastern Europe our schools are now teaching German, French, and English, just as they did before the war. Knowing these languages will help our young reach across our borders to build good relations as well as commerce. The countries of Europe are relatively small, and we will have to depend on one another and work together if we want to prosper."

Her comments reminded me that before and during the war we were taught both German and Czech and could elect to learn Italian or Latin as well; however, after the war we were not allowed to speak any language other than Czech. By the time I left the country in 1946, I spoke Czech fluently.

Once we were on the road again, Erwin mentioned how long he thought it would take to bring this country back to Western standards. "With the right leadership," he said, "I would guess that in about ten to fifteen years, they should be able to compete once again in the world market. But they have a lot of work ahead of them." Lilli agreed. Still thinking about the new educational system the waitress had told us about, Lilli added, "This family has the right attitude. In time, this country too will recover and progress."

I was thinking of our destination, my hometown of Brno, wondering whether or not I would be able to get the document I wanted. The more details I could uncover, the more connected I would feel. When I saw a sign for Hedwick's village of Žatčany, a small farming community outside of Brno, I wondered what she could teach me about our ancestors.

When we reached her home, Hedwick was standing outside, waiting for us with happy tears in her eyes. The last time I had seen her she was seventeen years old. She would come by our home in her school dress—a striped, navy blue dress with brass buttons and a sailor's collar—to pick up Lilli on her way to the library to study. The two of them, both about the same height, looked like twins with their matching long, chestnut brown hair.

Lilli was the first one to reach and embrace Hedwick. I noticed that their brown curls had turned to grey and that Lilli now stood a little taller than Hedwick, whose shoulders were stooped from years of hard work. Her eyes were still a deep brown though their twinkle had faded. Six-foot-tall Erwin looked like a giant next to her small and delicate frame and when I finally got to greet her I felt her rough, callused hands. "Welcome, welcome," she kept repeating over and over between her tears, "I am so happy to see all of you."

As we unloaded the car, Hedwick was overwhelmed by the many gifts we had brought her and her family. They all had come to welcome us and have dinner. Her daughter Dagmar had married an engineer and had two beautiful children, a boy and a girl, now teenagers attending college in Brno. The family lived only a few miles away, in one of the city suburbs. Overjoyed with the presents they received, the children immediately tried on the new jeans and shirts, which fit perfectly. Their happy and smiling faces were gratitude enough for us as they did not speak German and our knowledge of Czech was minimal.

Dinner reminded me of Mother's cooking; glazed carrots, potato dumplings, Brussels sprouts, cauliflower, sweet sour cabbage, roasted chicken, salads, and apple strudel had been prepared just as Mother used to. Hedi, as we affectionately called her, must have spent many hours in the kitchen to make our favorite foods from childhood. I had not tasted any Czech or Austrian food for years and had to sample everything. Conversation around the dinner table was a mixture of German and Czech as the children did not speak German very well and Dagmar and her husband didn't speak it at all; they had chosen to study French instead. Though we did not all share a language, we managed to navigate through years of memories—reminiscing, laughing, and crying. When we finally settled in for the night, it was late. Hedi slept on a sofa in her kitchen, I slept on a cot in the hallway, Erwin in the living room and Lilli in the bedroom.

Awakened by Hedi's early rising rooster, I looked out a window in the back of the house and saw about a dozen chickens in a coop within a small fenced in area around a tree stump where the rooster sat. Behind the coop were Hedi's small vegetable garden and a few small fruit trees. In the back of the garden, behind a couple of bee-hives, was a wood shed with garden supplies, tools, and stacks of wood for the fireplace. The walls of her small house were about eigh-teen inches thick, the windows very small, and the narrow doorways very low. Erwin had to duck every time he walked through one of them. Air conditioning was not needed, even in August, as the thick walls kept the house comfortably cool.

After breakfast, Erwin drove all of us into the city to the places close to our hearts. Tired of dodging the potholes, he suggested we park the car and walk. As we explored the streets, it seemed as if nothing had changed since 1946. Apartment buildings, department stores, and office buildings in the downtown area were all covered with traffic dust, and the pavements and sidewalks were in bad need of repair. I remembered that even during the war, the city employed street sweepers, and windows as well as the outside of buildings were periodically cleaned. The cobblestone streets, which inevitably had stones come loose, were kept in good condition. It seemed as if time had stood still since then. On our street, the buildings that had been razed by bombings or fire had not been rebuilt. The façades, surrounded by piles of bricks and rubble, remained just as we had left them.

Towards the end of the war, I had a frightening experience that suddenly came to me as I looked up at our apartment build-ing and saw bullet holes across the outside walls of the whole third floor. A British pilot of a low flying fighter plane used some of the taller, freestanding apartment buildings for target practice; my family's third floor apartment was in such a building. During one of his practices, I was sitting between two windows in our living room when his bullets just missed our windows.

"Look," I said to Lilli and Erwin, "the bullet holes are still there." Only the windowpanes had been replaced. We walked behind the apartment building and found the back wall still dirty and damaged from a fire caused by a bomb decades earlier. Erwin wanted to know whether I remembered the fire. "Oh, yes," I said, "I remember it very well, as if it happened yesterday." Then I told them of the bombing attack when a German soldier who had taken shelter during the bombing raid and I went up the three flights and rescued our neighbor and her baby. "I remember Frau Hoffman." Lilli commented. "Was she all right?" I then told them that although I was nearly suffocated by smoke on the last landing, everyone came through it all right. "I don't know what happened to Frau Hoffman after that," I said. "During the last days of the war everyone was preoccupied with how and where to survive the last conflict. We lost touch with her."

When we came back to the front of the building, I said with a sweeping motion of my hand, "This was like a ghost-town the last time I saw this street. We returned from the country and all we could see were Russian soldiers abducting women and plundering whatever they could." Close to tears, Lilli said, "I am sorry you have such bad memories. Maybe we should not have come."

I told both of them that this reunion with the past has had a cleansing effect on me. "But can you imagine," I asked, "the burdens on the hearts of those who have to live here and see these sites day in and day out?" Erwin and Lilli agreed it would be overwhelming. After walking a few more blocks we headed towards Hedi's home in the country. After dinner that evening, I told Hedi of my attempt to fill in our family pedigree chart, and she offered to take me to the city archives the next day to get my grandparents' marriage certificate.

Impatient to visit the archives, I awoke before the rooster and caught the first morning bus with Hedi. On the way I told her of the difficulties I had getting information through the Czech Embassy in Washington, D.C. "I am not surprised," she said, "Research was not possible three years ago for anyone who did not have govern-ment credentials." I did not understand. "You have no idea how the Communist regime scrutinized everything anybody did," Hedi continued. "All records were sealed."

As we approached the single-story archives building, I gave Hedi a questioning look. She read my mind. "This is not where all of our records are housed. Everything prior to a certain date is held in temperature-controlled vaults elsewhere. To obtain a document prior to a certain date, you have to place an order ahead of time."

We entered the building and learned that the records office was at the end of a long hallway. As Hedi and I approached the receptionist's window, I noticed the woman's stern look. Her hair was combed back in a military style and her face not showing any color or life, took me back to the Communist era. Hedi asked for the document we wanted to see. While waiting, I looked around. A long table with chairs filled the narrow but well-lit room; the only person on the far side was a young man busy copying from a book. When our document came, the middle-aged woman behind the window, without looking up, said to Hedi in a short and business-like manner, "That will be 30 Korunas." Hedi thanked the woman, paid the fee, and we sat down at the table opposite the young transcriber.

Hedi had to translate the document from Czech to German as I was no longer fluent in Czech. When we came to my grandfather's occupation, Hedi was not sure of the correct translation. The young man across the table looked up from his work and said in German that my grandfather had been an ironworker. Surprised to hear him speak to us in German, I said to him "Vielen Dank. Sie sprechen Deutsch?" (Thank you very much. Do you speak German?)

He nodded and I added, "I have been admiring what appears to be an ancient book from which you were transcribing. The scrolled colorful lettering fascinates me." He explained, "I am a student at Masaryck University, transcribing from sixteenth century Latin into Czech, using the translation for my finals."

Then I asked him something that had not occurred to me before. Looking back, I wonder whether I was inspired. "Do you know someone who would be interested in doing family research by correspondence? I am in the country for only a short time and had hoped to find someone here who also speaks English." I was surprised and delighted when he said without hesitation, "I do." I had come thousands of miles to get one document from the Brno archives only to find a researcher who not only spoke English, German and Czech but was willing to do research for me. I knew right then, it was not a coincidence.

We exchanged addresses and agreed to our financial terms. I left him with blank pedigree charts and family data. Correspondence started crossing the Atlantic almost immediately and within two years I had a fifteen-generation pedigree chart with direct lines completed to the sixteenth century. What an accomplishment. What a blessing!

As I held the finished chart in my hand a couple years later, I remembered Mother telling me as we sat in a shelter basement in 1945, with Russian troops on our doorsteps, that I had been an unwanted child. At the time I had been devastated: part of my heart went numb. But years later, with the charts in my hand and with God as my guide, sending me blessings after blessings during all adversity, I knew that He had a reason and a purpose for my coming into this world. I was willing to do whatever He had sent me here to do.

On the third and final day of our visit, Hedi and I, in anticipation of my visit to Pohořelice, picked a bouquet of flowers from her garden. She had heard of the Death March to Pohořelice and the mass grave in southern Moravia where hundreds of helpless people had been murdered and tossed into a ditch. I had the strength of mind to revisit this place and in humility ask God to help me understand the nature of war and learn of His justice.

Since the Wall had come down two years before, the new Czech government had built a modern highway between Brno and Vienna. The road it replaced served as a reminder not only of events in 1945, but also of Napoleon's march to Austerlitz a century earlier. It was now used only for local traffic and would soon be eliminated altogether. Erwin sensed that I preferred traveling the old road, the "Wiener Strasse," as it was called, potholes and all. He was right.

The tall chestnut trees that once flanked both sides of the road and had given shelter to so many exhausted and dying elderly on May 31, 1945, had been cut down; the wide, shallow ditches, resting places for those who could go no farther at the time, were still visible. At that time the road seemed to have no end; neither did the suffering of those thousands walking the road into uncertainty.

Erwin drove without speaking, respecting my need for reflection. After an hour we reached the outskirts of Pohořelice and the now abandoned grounds of the former State Agricultural Experimental Station with its huge storage buildings still visible in the distance. He stopped by the side of the road. A twenty-foot tall black steel cross faced the field in front of the road. A plaque hung at the foot of the cross with two benches on either side. I saw a woman placing flowers there and I told Erwin it was time for me to pay my respects. "I know you want to be alone," he said. "We'll be back in an hour." The moment I had been waiting for so long had come. As I looked over the field of freshly planted clover, I could not help thinking of the hundreds of bodies buried beneath it.

I placed my flowers at the cross, nodded a greeting to the woman sitting on one of the benches and sat beside her. I felt the need to talk to her but did not know what language she spoke. Pointing to the field of clover below the cross, I asked her in German whether she had lost someone who had been buried there. "No," she answered in broken German, "but I know the history of what happened here. Every year on my father's death date I come here and honor him this way." I did not understand what she meant. She went on to explain: "My father used to keep meticulously accurate burial records for the town and at the time this massacre happened, he made sure that everyone's identity and cause of death in this mass grave were identified. He always believed and taught me that every human being is worthy of honor." *Amazing*, I thought, remembering that after the war giving Germans dignity or respect had been dangerous.

She continued, "A month or two after my father filled in the ledger, it disappeared and when it mysteriously showed up again, twelve pages, with the people's names buried in this field of clover, were missing. My father did not remember all the names that were missing, but he knew that on those twelve pages had been the names of close to nine-hundred men, women, and children."

What a great man her father must have been, passing his principles of honesty and respect on to his child. I wished I could have met him. I introduced myself to her and told her that I knew what had happened here as well, because my mother and I were here on that tragic day in 1945. I had come to pay my respects to my fellow countrymen and find an answer. She asked about my mother. I told her, "She passed away in Germany, after we were expelled from our homeland."

"I am very sorry about all that happened after the war and to you for the loss of your mother and home. It was not right for the government to expel all the people, particularly the elderly. My father said that many times while he was alive," she said.

I thanked her and then asked her about the cross. She explained that at first, under the Communist regime, it was illegal to place flowers or candles at the site. "Occasionally," she continued, "drivers in foreign-tagged cars would drive by and throw flowers down the embankment. The Communists wanted us to forget what happened here, but who can forget so many innocent, mistreated, and killed human beings," she said. "After the Iron Curtain came down, an Austrian humanitarian organization erected the cross and placed the memorial."

Then she looked at me and asked: "What answer are you trying to find here? Do you mind sharing the question with me?" I said, "I have come to ask if God can forgive those who participated in the atrocities that happened here." She looked at me and after a moment said, "I pray for all of them every day." I felt touched by her response. As we said goodbye, I thanked the woman for the opportunity to have met her. "I promise you," I said to her, "that I will speak up for those whose voices had been silenced so many years ago." She took both of my hands in hers and said, "Thank you."

I closed my eyes and thanked the Lord in deep humility for the opportunity to be here. "My past has made me what I am today," I prayed, "and I am grateful for that past because it has helped me appreciate life in its simplest terms. I have experienced hunger and plenty, hate and joy, laughter and tears. All these things have so abundantly enriched my life that my cup runneth over. For that I am deeply grateful."

I went on and asked the Lord for His blessings upon the souls of those who had gone so many years before, the silent dead whose voices were not heard and whose remains were buried in the field where I stood. I asked for His insight and understanding of World War II and its aftermath. Then finally, I asked the question I had held close in my heart for decades: "Is the torture and killing of innocent people forgivable by Thee and how, after all these years, can I find healing after all the pain I experienced?" I sat there quietly, waiting to hear an answer. Soon I felt an impression on my heart and mind; the words were clear: "No leader should rule unjustly over his people, but only I will be the judge of all nations and their rulers and my judgment will be just."

Then I asked to understand the hate and discrimination I experienced. He assured me, "I will also judge them fairly for I know the true intents of their hearts."

As these words touched my soul, I remembered Him leading my Mother and me out of this camp so many years earlier and laying a calming blanket over my heart. "Be still," He had whispered, "I have everything under control." So many times since then had I seen His power and felt His compassion. As I stood by the field of clover, I asked, "How can I and my fellow man, thinking of all those who suffered here and others who suffered under the Nazi regime, find healing in our hearts?"

His answer came quickly: "Healing comes through forgiveness." Again, I felt the words reaching my heart, and I knew then why God had wanted me to come here to get His answers: To open my eyes to the beautiful and free new homeland He had blessed me with and to let me experience the cleansing effect of letting go of the past where the haunting atrocities had occurred.

By bringing me to His Church ten years ago, He had taught me His doctrine of love and forgiveness. As a result, and by returning to my homeland, I no longer carried any bitterness in my heart and I am finally able to fully forgive my countrymen. As I researched my family's lineage and wrote my people's history, I could see why God had given me the responsibility to do what my older sister Margita could not.

I had crossed to the other side of knowing. At last, I was at peace and free to do what I was sent to do.

The memorial at Pohořelice on Highway 461,
between Brno and Vienna honors the victims
of a massacre that occurred at this site.

Epilogue

OVER TWENTY YEARS HAVE PASSED since my trip to my native country and my visit to the field of the silent dead near Pohořelice. The experience had a lasting effect.

About ten years ago, my siblings passed away without knowing that my promise to them, writing this history, would soon be realized. Their wish, for their children and grandchildren to learn of our family's past struggles, will soon become reality.

My husband Ray and I maintained a wonderful relationship the last ten years until his sudden death in 1990.

It is my hope that our posterity and you, my reader, will embrace the lessons that I have learned throughout my life and by that field of clover: "Healing comes through forgiveness."

"Be still, and know that I am God."
Psalm 46:10

Made in the USA
San Bernardino, CA
11 February 2017